HEINEMANN TEXT PROCESSING

for modular awards

LEGAL TEXT PROCESSING

STAGE II

HELEN SALISBURY & BARBARA EDWARDS

Heinemann Educational Publishers,
Halley Court, Jordan Hill, Oxford OX2 8EJ
A division of Reed Educational & Professional Publishing Ltd

Heinemann is a registered trademark of Reed Educational & Professional Publishing Limited

OXFORD MELBOURNE AUCKLAND
JOHANNESBURG BLANTYRE GABORONE
IBADAN PORTSMOUTH NH (USA) CHICAGO

First published 1998
2002 2001 2000 99
10 9 8 7 6 5 4 3

A catalogue for this book is available from the British Library on request.

ISBN 0 435 45391 2

Designed by Jackie Hill

Typeset by TechType, Abingdon, Oxon

Printed and bound in Great Britain by Athenaeum Press Ltd, Gateshead, Tyne and Wear

Contents

About this book

This book provides coverage of the RSA Legal Text Processing Stage II Part 2 examination. It is also suitable for legal text processing and secretarial examinations offered by other awarding bodies. It is anticipated that users of this book will have achieved or be working towards RSA Text Processing Stage II Part 1 and RSA Word Processing Stage II Part 2 awards.

The vocabulary used for explanations is kept as simple as possible.

The book is divided into three sections:

■ 1 General Theory

This section provides information on special requirements for working in the legal environment and also for the examination itself.

■ 2 Exercises

This section is broken down into six sections, each dealing with a specific department of a large legal practice (reception, property, probate, litigation, corporate services and general office). In these exercises, you will take the part of a legal secretary working for Edwards, Brook and Cole, Solicitors based in Midsomer Norton near Bath. In this role, you will start as a junior legal secretary in the reception area. As you progress through the book you will work as legal secretary to a partner in each of the different departments of the practice. These exercises will provide you with practice in keying in the different types of document that you are likely to come across in the legal environment.

■ 3 Exam Practice

This section provides you with 5 mock examination papers as well as hints and tips for sitting your examination.

Format of the book

The exercises in this book are presented in handwritten draft as well as typewritten. This type of presentation is practised in the examination as well as in the workplace. Some of the tasks may be more demanding than those you will meet in the examinations. This will help you to develop your confidence and ability to succeed in the examination, as well as preparing you for working in the legal environment.

Letterheads, memos and blank pre-printed forms for use with the exercises throughout this book can be found at the back of the book on pages 106–122. You may photocopy these for use with this book. Alternatively, your tutor may provide you with templates for letterheads, memos and forms.

Worked examples for all the mock examination papers are included at the end of the book on pages 95–105.

House style

Each legal practice will have its own house style – ie way of laying out documents. In the case of Edwards, Brook and Cole, all documents should be fully blocked – ie each new paragraph should start at the left-hand side. Letters should use the open punctuation style – ie only blocks of text should be punctuated; there should be no punctuation in the address block, references or salutation.

If there is an enclosure or enclosures to be sent with a letter or memo, the abbreviation *Enc* or *Encs* should be typed two spaces below the last line.

When an extra copy of a letter has to be sent, the abbreviation *cc* should be added, together with any routing information two spaces below the enclosure abbreviation or last line. An original and two copies of the letter should be printed (or two photocopies of the original made), and a tick placed after the appropriate entry on each copy. The third copy will be a file copy. The following example shows how each copy would be marked:

Original
Encs

cc Accounts Department
File

Copy 1
Encs

cc Accounts Department ✓
File

Copy 2
Encs

cc Accounts Department
File ✓

Note to tutors

If students are working on word processors rather than typewriters, you may prefer to provide them with templates for the letterheads, memos and forms. If so, you – or the students – will need to key them in. Alternatively, you can photocopy the ones provided at the back of the book (pages 106–122) and the students can then print on to these.

General Theory

Introduction to legal terminology

As you work through this book, and certainly if you get work in a legal office, you will meet many new words and phrases. Whether you are using a word processor or a typewriter, it would be a good idea to buy a legal dictionary. These are printed by the specialist legal publishers and a good bookshop should have a copy or be able to order one for you.

If you work in a legal office and use a word processor then you may find that many of these legal words and terms have been added to the dictionary on the software. This is very likely if you are using a computer that is linked to a network. If you are using a stand-alone computer, then the previous job holder may have done this for you. Whichever is the case, as you come across new words, it is a good idea to add them to the dictionary to help you in the future. Before you do this, however, check with your supervisor, or – if you are at college – ask your tutor for advice.

If you are working for a small firm of solicitors or in chambers (ie preparing documentation for use in courts) you will soon become familiar with a wide range of legal vocabulary. If you are a secretary working in a large organisation, you may find yourself in a specialist department and become very knowledgeable about this aspect of legal work. Some typical legal departments may include:

- Litigation (cases that go to court), which includes:
  - Family Law (matrimonial cases – separation, divorce, maintenance and custody of children)
- Property (conveyancing work and tenancy agreements)
- Probate (wills and settling of estates after death)
- Corporate Services (company law)

To help you to build up your legal vocabulary:

- keep a notebook and add new words and phrases as you meet them, *and*
- if there is anything you do not understand, ask your supervisor – or the person who gave you the task – to explain.

Keying in legal text

It is difficult to give specific rules for setting out tasks as each legal practice will have its own way of laying out documents.

- Be aware of the different ways of setting documents out.
- Be prepared to adapt to suit the ways of your employer.
- It is very important, in legal documents, that everything is clear and free from errors.
- Be *consistent* within a document.

Line spacing

The vocabulary and content of legal documents can be very complicated. Double line spacing is often used to help all concerned to read and understand the document.

Spaced capitals

Some words are emphasised in documents by using spaced capitals. The following examples show words and phrases that might be in spaced capitals:

T H I S   A G R E E M E N T
W H E R E A S
B E T W E E N
I N   W I T N E S S

To key in spaced capitals:

- tap the space bar once between each letter, *and*
- 3 times between each word.

If these words occur in the middle of a sentence:

- leave 3 spaces before the words in spaced capitals, *and*
- 3 spaces after them.

Note: If you are using a word processor, spaced capitals may not always look clear in your printed work – it will depend on the type of font you are using.

Capitals

Other words are typed in capitals. These are often directives (instructions for carrying out items). The following examples show words that are often typed in capitals:

SIGNED SEALED AND DELIVERED
SIGNED
I REVOKE
I APPOINT
I GIVE AND BEQUEATH
PROVIDED ALWAYS

The names of people may also be typed in capitals the first time they appear in a legal document.

Emboldening and underlining

Words or phrases in legal documents may also be emphasised by emboldening or underlining. The following examples show words that have been emboldened or underlined:

BETWEEN
<u>STATUTORY DECLARATION</u>

In the examination, you may be asked to emphasise a word or a heading. In this case, you may choose which method to use, and italics is an acceptable alternative. You may also use a combination of more than one style. The following examples show various styles:

WITNESS STATEMENT
<u>WITNESS STATEMENT</u>
<u>*WITNESS STATEMENT*</u>

Initial capitals

Some words will usually be keyed in using initial capitals if they refer to a specific document:

... this Deed ...
... this Conveyance ...

but:

deeds are complicated documents

conveyances can sometimes be confusing

In this book, and in the examination, you should follow the style given in the draft material. In the workplace, you will learn which words need initial capitals and which do not. However, if you are unsure, you should always check with your supervisor.

Punctuation and numbered or lettered items

Some legal documents, including a Deed or Transfer of Property, may not contain any punctuation. This is to make sure that there is no misinterpretation of the content of the document. In these cases, the general practice is that you should not:

✗ put full stops or commas in sentences
✗ put full stops after numbered or lettered items, *or*
✗ break up names and addresses with commas.

Remember, though, that legal offices may differ in how they lay documents out so you should always follow the draft as closely as possible and ask if you are unsure of anything.

Witness statements may have full stops after numbered items and in sentences; they are a statement of facts as known by the client. Items covering employment law may contain full stops.

Different examples are used throughout this book. In this book, and in the examination, you should follow the draft. In the workplace, you will learn which documents need punctuation and which do not and practice may vary between offices. However, if you are unsure, you should always ask your supervisor.

Signing documents

Most legal documents have to be signed and some must be witnessed (ie one or more people sign and date the document and two other people confirm that they have seen it being signed). The witnesses' signatures will be added to the document together with their names printed in capitals and details of their occupation and address.

Sometimes a brace will be used to bracket together the details of a person signing a legal document. The brace is usually created using single line spacing, and this can be achieved by setting a tab stop to align the brackets as in the following example:

SIGNED by the above named HENRY)
JOSEPH LAPINSKY in our presence)
and by us in his)

Mr Lapinsky would sign in the space on the right-hand side of the document.

Continuation sheets

Each legal practice will have its own way of producing continuation sheets for legal documents. Some solicitors prefer pages to be numbered to improve the organisation of their work. If this is the case:

- do not number page one, *but*
- begin numbering with page two.

The preferred style is to put the number as a figure in the bottom centre of each continuation sheet.

If business letters extend to a continuation sheet, any second and subsequent sheets should be numbered, and this is sufficient for RSA examinations.

Using legal forms and documents

Many legal documents and forms are now stored on disk on computer. In a large organisation, these computers may be networked and all departments might have access to a whole range of documentation. The partners of the firm will have:

- discussed the content and layout of these documents, *and*
- agreed on 'precedents' (ie a method that has worked well in the past and will therefore be adopted for the future).

The solicitor dealing with each client will instruct the secretary on how to amend the document to meet the needs of each individual case.

Note: A major source of reference for all organisations involved in legal work is the *Encyclopaedia of Forms and Precedents* (some 40 plus volumes in size) which is published by Butterworths & Co.

Some legal forms and documents will be bought in from specialist legal stationers. Many can now be put onto disk but some items, for example court forms, still need to be typed on to the original printed form and a typewriter is essential.

Corrections to legal documents are not allowed and photocopies are not legally acceptable. However, photocopies are often given to clients for their reference, while the original is stored in the solicitor's storage room.

Security and confidentiality when working in a legal office

When you start work you will be asked to sign a Contract of Employment. This must be provided by all employers, and will almost certainly contain a section that refers to confidentiality. This will ask you to agree not to disclose any confidential information about the company, its business, its trade secrets or the details of any client with whom you are dealing as part of your job. This confidentiality will extend even after you have left your particular employment.

When using a word processor or typewriter, always make sure you follow good office practice:

- do not leave papers and folders lying around
- put items away when not in use
- use screen savers or switch to a blank document when visitors are around, *and*
- shred any spoilt sheets.

If you use a word processor, you will have your own personal password to allow you to use your computer or to access the network. This password should not be disclosed to anyone else. The solicitor or legal practitioner for whom you are working will probably be able to access the documents via his or her own password.

Abbreviations

The following standard abbreviations should be typed as they appear in the document. Their meanings are given to help you understand them. Key them in for practice and future reference.

Abbreviation	**Meaning**
etc	and so on
eg	for example
ie	that is
NB	take notice of what follows
PS	an additional paragraph at the end of a letter after the signature
v	against – eg Jones v Smith
All ER	All England Law Reports
QC	Queen's Counsel
plc	public limited company
Ltd	limited liability of a private or public company
&	and

The following standard abbreviations should always be keyed in in full. Commonly-used legal abbreviations will be shown at the end of each department in Section 2 and in the glossary at the back of the book (page 123).

Days of the week

Mon	Monday
Tues	Tuesday etc

Months of the year

Jan	January
Feb	February etc

Words in addresses

Rd	Road	St	Street
Ave	Avenue	Dr	Drive
Sq	Square	Cres	Crescent
Pl	Place	Pk	Park

Complimentary closes

ffly	faithfully
sincly	sincerely

Correction signs

You will need to know what the following correction signs mean in order to make the necessary amendments to text.

New paragraph	// or [	Start a new paragraph
Run on		Continue to type on the same line, ignore the paragraph break.
Insertion		Insert the circled words exactly where the insertion sign points – be careful to note where any punctuation may be. For example, you may have to insert a number of words before a comma or full stop that is already on the page – make sure you don't forget to include it.
Transpose horizontally		Move the words around so that the last section becomes the first word to type.
or balloon with arrow Transpose vertically	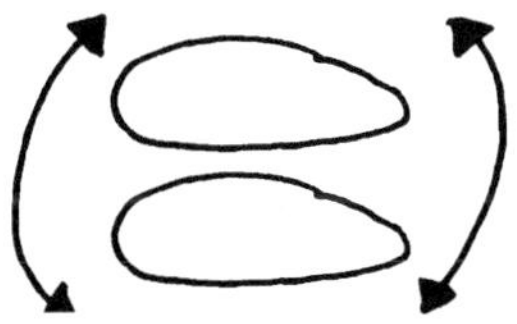	This means you have to change the line on which the words/figures are typed. Remember to look at the arrows carefully – you should only move text that is directly covered by the arrows.
Close up		This means you should remove any extra spaces.
Leave a space		Leave a space wherever this sign appears.
stet		This means that you should type only the words that have a dotted line underneath them.
in the margin:		

Proofreading your work

It is very important to read through your finished work very carefully. In the examination, one of the most common reasons for failure is accuracy faults. In the workplace, it is vital to be accurate, particularly in a legal office where any inaccuracy can lead to misinterpretation.

- Always use the correct fingers when keying in work, which will enable you to concentrate on the draft material in front of you.
- When you have finished keying in a task, always read the work on screen – or on the paper if you are using a typewriter.
- If you have a spellchecker facility, make sure that you use it – remember though, that although it will find misspelt words and keying errors, it will not find wrong words that are spelt correctly (eg *grate* instead of *great*).
- Do a final check against the draft material (or examination paper) when you have printed your work.
- Note any errors on the printed copy using a pen or pencil.

If you are using a word processor:

- recall the document to screen
- make the corrections
- reprint.

If you are using a typewriter correct the errors by:

- using a suitable correcting material (such as matching coloured correcting fluid, chalk paper or a hard rubber), *and*
- typing the correct characters – this is much easier to do with the paper still in the typewriter, because it is more difficult to align the work after reinserting the paper.

Alternatively, you may choose to retype the sheet. Remember though, that if you do this, you run the risk of making new errors.

Note: A document with corrections is not legally admissible. However, in the examination any corrections made will be accepted as long as they are neat and not too obvious.

Read the following three documents and try to find all the errors. When you think that you have found them all, check your answers against the key at the back of the book (page 94).

Proofreading Exercise 1

SALIS & BURY
Solicitors
23 Demontfort Road
Leicester LE3 9JR

Tel: 0116 278 4433
Fax: 0116 278 2211

Our ref DH/Minchin/KM

Allied Building Society
18 Marble Rd
Manchester
M42 1RY

Dear Sirs

The late Arthur William Minchin
Account Number M969354

I am sorry to inform you of the death on 30 May 1997 of Arthur William Minchin of 34 Archer Avenue, Market Bosworth, Leicestershire, LE12 3TY.

I am dealing with the winding-up of his est and enclose a certified copy of the Death Certificate for your inspection.

Could you please advice me of the balance in the above account as at the date of death, including interest accrued to that date but not credited, and provide me with a withdrawal form in respect of the account.

Please let me know if you require site of a Grant of Representation before releasing any funds and if you require any other docs to be submitted to you.

Yours faithfully

Donald Hickey

Proofreading Exercise 2

THIS IS THE LAST WILL AND TESTAMENT

of me

HENRY JOSEPH LAPINSKY of 12 The Ringway Howgreen in the County of Essex which I make this day of 199

1 I HEREBY REVOKE all previous wills and codls I have made. This is my last Will. As executers of this my will I appoint my wife Margaret Rose Lapinsky and my brother Barry Charles Lapinsky of The Old Vicarage Main Street How green Essex 2 I DIRECT that all my debts and funeral and testamentary expenses be paid as soon as is convenient after my death

3 I GIVE all my estate to my wife Margaret rose Lapinsky of 12 The Ringway Howgreen Essex as long as she survives me by 28 days. If she does not survive me by twenty-eight days I leave all my estate to my daughter Mrs Sandra Ruth Knight of 42 Bishops Drive Saltfleet Lincolnshire

IN WITNESS of which I have set my hand to this my will this day of 199

SIGNED by the above named HENRY)
JOSEPH LAPINSKY in our presence)
and by us in his)

(1st witness)
Name
of
Occupation

(2nd witness)
Name
of
Occupation

Exercises

Reception

You work as a junior legal secretary in the reception area. As the receptionist, your main responsibilities will be to greet all visitors and to operate the telephone switchboard. You may also be given simple tasks by members of staff from any of the departments.

The documents you are likely to come across in reception are general administrative ones that you would meet in other secretarial jobs. For example, memos, lists, notices, letters. You are unlikely to come across specific legal documents at this level.

Although you will not be processing complex pieces of work at the moment, you may come across some abbreviations which you are not familiar with. The most likely ones are listed below, and you should always type them in full. Your vocabulary will grow as you progress through the different departments in the partnership.

benefl	beneficial	something that has a helpful or useful effect
insolvt(cy)	insolvent(cy)	a person who cannot pay his/her debts (ie money he/she owes)
pceedg(s)	proceeding(s)	the steps taken in bringing a problem or claim before a court of law for settlement

New words that you may come across in this department are listed below with their meanings and derivations.

Breach of Court Order	Disobeying a Court Order
Epitome	A summary
Judicature	Relating to the administration of justice
Land Registry	The Land Registry keeps a record of land and whom it is owned by
Legal Aid	Free legal advice for people who earn less than a certain amount
Legal tender	Currency that can be used to pay for goods, services etc
Maintenance	The money a husband or wife pays after a divorce to support the ex-partner or a child
Parchment	A type of stiff, yellowish paper sometimes used for legal documents

Reception Exercise 1

EDWARDS, BROOKS AND COLE SOLICITORS

INTERNAL TELEPHONE DIRECTORY

John Edwards	Senior Partner Conveyancing	10
Ernest Mullins	Senior Partner Litigation	14
Jenny Brooks	Senior Partner Probate	18
Maurice Stand	Senior Partner Legal Aid	12
Catherine Whitby	Senior Partner Accounts	16
Andrew Cole	Senior Partner Corporate Services	13
Margaret Field	Partner Litigation	11
Michael Bond Band	Partner Corporate Services	20
Paul White	Partner Probate	19
Anthony Turner	Partner Litigation	15
Tina Longworth	Partner Conveyancing	22
Barbara Sinah	Partner Conveyancing	17
General Office	Roy Patel	21
General Office	Debbie Parsons	27
General Office	Laura Chapman	25
General Office	Janice Lloyd	23
General Office	Marie Bartlett	24
General Office	Jon Ching	26
Your name	Receptionist	30
June Dixon	Accounts Department	28
Timothy Wong	Accounts Department	29

Please rearrange this list into alphabetical order of Departments, eg

ACCOUNTS

June Dixon 28
Catherine Whitby 16
etc

CONVEYANCING

John Edwards 10
Tina Longworth 22
etc

Type in double line spacing making the Directory easy to read but attractively displayed

Reception Exercise 2

APPOINTMENT BOOK				
Monday (insert today's date)				
Name of caller	**Company**	**Time of arrival**	**To see**	**Department**
Matthew Henderson	Watts Legal Stationers	0900	Laura Chapman	General Office

Following the layout above, type the following in order of time and put in the appropriate Department from your internal telephone directory.

Mr and Mrs T Donaldson to see John Edwards at 9.15am

Debra Owen at 1030 to see Maurice Stand

Henry Osbourne from Bath Valuations at 0945 to see Barbara Sinah

Martin Letts at 11am from Midland Bank to see Timothy Wong

Mr and Mrs J Whittaker at 1000 to see Jenny Brook

Mrs Sylvia Lang from Morrison and Co to see Andrew Cole at 9.30am

Miss Tracy Evans at 12noon to see Ernest Mullins

Jeremy Colbourne from Jones and Walker at 1400 to see Michael Band.

Susan Riddle to see Margaret Field at 12.30pm

Mr and Mrs P Broad at 1600 to see Tina L——

William Cooke and Helen Smart to see John Edwards at 1530.

Reception Exercise 3

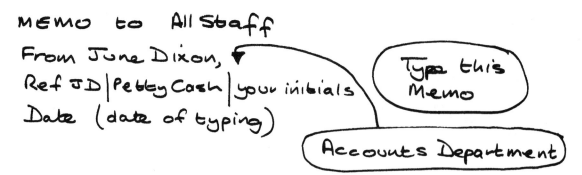

MEMO to All Staff

From June Dixon, Accounts Department

Ref JD|Petty Cash|your initials

Date (date of typing)

Type this Memo

Petty Cash Vouchers

Emphasise heading

Could all staff please ensure they obtain a receipt for all goods bought and attach this to the p— c— v—. All vouchers must be authorised by a supervisor. In future, anyone requesting money from petty cash without an authorised voucher will not be given any petty cash.

I take this opportunity to remind you all that cash is legal tender and is therefore very valuable. Our petty cash is ~~kept~~ in a lockable box and kept in the safe in the Accounts Department. All staff should be aware of their responsibilities and should, at all times, observe our in-house security regulations and procedures.

Reception Exercise 4

MEMO

To All Staff

From Janice Lloyd, General Office

Ref JL/your initials

Date (date of typing)

Type this Memo

HEALTH AND SAFETY

As you all know, I am the H— and S— Officer for our building. We have just had a new accident report book delivered and it will be kept in Reception together with the First Aid box. // Please ensure you report all accidents in the book, however minor they may appear. An example of the page layout of the book is shown below.

Date	Time	Name and department	Accident or illness and treatment (if any)

Please familiarise yourself with the headings and ensure the book is completed correctly.

Please put in the first incident we have had as an example. Use today's date. At 0935 Jon Ching from the General Office tripped on frayed carpet in the door way to Filing Room and hurt his knee. He was taken to the local Surgery.

2

Reception Exercise 5

MEMORANDUM

To Marie Bartlett General Office

From Timothy Wong

Reference TW/ (your initials)

Date (Date of typing)

PAYING-IN SLIPS FOR BANKING ← Underline this heading

Could I please remind you to take care when filling in these slips and ensure that ALL details are correct. The counterfoil must also be completed. You have omitted to do this on the last two occasions.

In future please ensure you have completed:-

1 The date of paying in to the bank

2 The amount paid in

← Rearrange numbers

3 The name of the person paying in

4 List all cheques with name and amount on the reverse of the paying-in slip (this breakdown allows us to check our entries)

5 Treat postal orders and money orders in the same way as cheques in 4) above.

Reception Exercise 6

MEMORANDUM

From Laura Chapman to Roy Patel using the appropriate initials and date

Type this Memo

Use the heading "Stationery" and suitably emphasise same.

Matthew Henderson from Watts Legal Stationers will be coming to see me at 9am on Monday (insert date for last Monday of the present month).

Would you please ~~up-date~~ complete the attached stationery checklist for me by then.

I need to know how many of each item we still have in stock – you can take the figures from the stock cards and just do a random check on some items to ensure the cards are up-to-date.

Key in the Legal Stationery Check List making the appropriate amendments

Reception Exercise 7

Retain all abbreviations

LEGAL STATIONERY CHECK LIST			
Parchment		**Conveyancing**	
A4 Fly Headed		Notice of Assignment	
A4 Covers		Req on Title	
A4 Single Headed		Pre-Contract Enquiries	
16 x 21 Headed		Conveyancing Questionnaires	
MM Will Paper		Con Check List	
A4 Fly Headed		Con 29 (1994)	
F/Cap Fly Headed		Stand Cond	
Demy Headed		Transaction	
Plain Engrossing		CR21	
A4 Blue or Cream		LLCI	
F/Cap Blue or Cream		Epitome	
Demy Blue or Cream		Sched of Docs	
Word Processing 100 gsm		Con Q4	
A4 White Plain /120		**Agreements**	
A4 Cream Plain		Exclusivity	
A4 White Will & Test		**Land Registry**	
A4 White Will Blk Marg 2pp		1B	
A4 White Blk Marg 1pp		19 DFT	
A4 White Red Marg 2pp		19	
~~Brother 7020~~		19 (Co)	
Judicature		19 (Co) DFT	
A4 Fly Ruled		19 (JP)	
A4 Single Plain		19 (JP) DFT	
A4 Fly Plain		20	
F/Cap Single Plain		20 DFT	
F/Cap Fly Plain		53	
Printing		53 (Co)	
Letterheads		63/14	
Professional Charges		94A	
Compliment Slips		96	
Business Cards		A4	
Printed Covers		A5	
Printed Envelopes		A13	
Legal Sundries		109	
China Grass		A4 White Red Marg 1pp	
Silk Tape			
Pink Tape			
Deed Gusset			
Company Seals			
Taxation Paper			

Reception Exercise 8

Draft from Maurice Stand, for typing please

our firm has recently been successfully approved by the Legal Aid Board and we have now received our logo to put in our window to show we are franchised as such. This logo will also be included in our stationery when we next have some printed.

From the following notes, would you please type up an error free copy that can be used in Reception to let people know more about L — A — and how benefl it may be to them.

LEGAL AID ← Centre and emphasise heading

If you are on a low or modest income and have little or no capitol you may qualify for L — A —. Telephone first to make an appointment stating that you will need Legal Advice and Assistance, to help you with your problem. You may just need general advice on legal problems such as divorce, maintenance, debt or immigration matters. Other typical problems fall into the following categories: personal injury, insolvcy, crime, family and housing and welfare benefits. We will be able to tell you at once whether you qualify for this help without paying any contribution or not. This type of Legal Aid is often called the Green Form Scheme and this will be explained to you fully when you make your first visit.

If you need to go to court in civil pceedgs we may advise you to apply for Civil Legal Aid or in some cases we may advise Assistance by Way of Representation which covers the cost of us preparing your case and representing you in most civil cases in magistrates' courts. It will also be available to anyone facing imprisonment in the magistrates' court for non-payment of a fine or charge or for breach of a court order.

Please type this from the heading LEGAL AID and I will add to it later

Property

You work as a legal secretary to John Edwards who is the senior partner in the Conveyancing Department. The work in this department will include matters relating to the transfer of ownership of land or property both freehold and leasehold. It will also include Landlord and Tenant rental agreements.

The documents you are likely to come across in this department are:

- Title Deeds – these are documents that prove someone owns a property. They are usually typed with spaces left for signatures.
- HM Land Registry Forms – these are forms which are used to carry out property searches when someone is buying a property. They are forms and must be completed very clearly and carefully.
- Conveyances – these are documents which transfer the ownership of land or property. They are usually typed with spaces left for signatures and dates.
- Tenancy Agreements – these are documents which set out the rights and responsibilities of both the landlord and tenant in the case of rented property. They are usually typed with spaces left for signatures.
- Leases – these are long-term tenancies (sometimes for periods of 99 years). The person leasing the property will pay either an annual rent or a large capital sum at the beginning and then a small annual ground rent. These are set out in a similar way to tenancy agreements.
- Standard documents such as letters and memos – these will be similar to letters and memos that you would type in any other office. However, the language is likely to be more complex.

In the course of your work in this department, you may come across some abbreviations which you are not familiar with. The most likely ones are listed below, and you should always type them in full.

clt(s)	client(s)	a person using the services of a lawyer
contt(s)	contract(s)	a formal agreement between 2 parties
convce(s)	conveyance(s)	a document which transfers the legal ownership of land or property
covt(s)	covenant(s)	a formal agreement
dft(s)	draft(s)	a rough copy
doc(s)	document(s)	a piece of paper giving information or evidence
est	estate	all a person owns and is left at his/her death
pchs(r)	purchase or purchaser	to buy/the buyer
ppty	property	items which are owned
solr	solicitor	a lawyer who advises clients and instructs barristers

New words that you may come across in this department are listed below with their meanings and derivations.

Aforesaid	Spoken of before	
Aggregate	Total	
Annexed	Added to	
Assign	To legally transfer property	assignable assignee assignor

Completion	When property or land changes hand after signing contracts	
Covenant (vb)	To agree	
Delineated	Drawn/outlined	
Easement	The right of someone other than the owner to benefit from the land, eg a right of way	
Exception and reservation	The creation of an easement to benefit the vendor, eg keeping the right to walk/drive across the land being sold	
Guarantee	A promise to do something	guarantor
Hereby	By means of/as a result of this	
Herein	In this point/document	
Hereinafter	From this point on	
Hereto	To this place, document, etc	
Hereunto	To this place, document etc	
Incumbrance	When someone else has an interest in the land, eg a mortgage or a lease	
Indemnified against	Secured/protected against	
In pursuance of	Following/in agreement with	
Lease	A contract allowing the use of land or a building for a set time	leasehold leaseholder
Mortgage	A loan for buying a property – the property is also used as security	mortgagee a mortgagor/er
Purchaser	Buyer	
Restrictions	Limits	
Seised of	Are the legal owners of	
Situate (adj)	Situated	
Stipulations	Guarantees, promises	
Surveyor	An official who checks buildings or land in order to give it a price	
Thereto	To that or it	
Title Deeds	Documents that prove someone owns a property	
Transactions	Agreements/negotiations	
Transfer	To convey or make over the ownership of or rights in a property from one party to another	transferee transference transferor/er
Trustee	A person managing the estate of a dead person or of someone not old enough to be legally responsible him/herself	
Vendor	Seller	
Whereas	It being the case that; since	
Whereof	Of which	
Witness	A person who gives evidence in a court of law *or* A person who confirms another person's signature	

Property Exercise 1

our ref JE/your initials

Mr and Mrs T Gregson
49 Silver Birch Ave
Midsomer Norton
BATH
BA3 2LJ

Dear Mr and Mrs Gregson

RE: SALE OF 49 SILVER BIRCH AVENUE

Thank you for your instructions to act in the sale of the above-mentioned ppty. I confirm that we shall be very pleased to act for you.

Would you please let us have ~~We need to have a copy of~~ the Title Deeds of your property. If you do not ~~have~~ hold these yourself, would you please let us have your Building Society name and your Roll or Account number.

We enclose a Property Information form togethers with a Fixtures and Fittings form for you to complete and return to me by give date for first Mon of next month.

I look forward to hearing from you.

Yours sncly

John Edwards

Property Exercise 2

2

Our ref JE/your initials

> Top plus 2 please. One for Barbara Sinah and one for File. Indicate routing

Mr and Mrs T Gregson
49 Silver Birch Ave
Midsomer Norton
BATH
BA3 2LJ

Dear Mr and Mrs Gregson

re: Purchase of 75 Parkland Way ← Emphasise this heading

I write to confirm that I have received a letter from your proposed (Seller's) solr confirming that they are awaiting receipt of their clts' Title Deeds. When these are received they will forward the Dft Contt to me.

In addition to the local Search that has to be carried out on your purchase, we also have to carry out a Coal Board Search on all properties in this area.

When I have received the Draft Contract I will contact ~~I have today written to~~ the local Coal Board surveyor asking him to carry out this Search.

These Searches are to establish if there is anything which may (adversley) ~~affect~~ effect the ppty you are buying. // I will be in contact with you again as soon as I receive the Contract.

Yours sncly

John Edwards

Property Exercise 3

Our ref JE|your initials

Mr and Mrs T Gregson
49 Silver Birch Ave
Midsomer Norton
BATH
BA3 2LJ

Dear Mr and Mrs Gregson

RE: PURCHASE OF 45 PARKLAND WAY

I/am pleased to confirm exchange of contracts with a completion date of (give date for last Fri of next month).

Would you please arrange with the Seller for the collection of the keys on the (days) of completion. Also ensure you have a buildings insurance for the property from now onwards. Your Building Society will normally undertake this for you. From the date you move into the property you ~~will need~~ may also wish to have a contents insurance.

You will need to (arange) with the electricity, gas and telephone authorities for their services to be available in your new property from the date of completion.

Yours sncly

John Edwards

(The draft convce has been sent to the Vendor's (Seller's) solicitors for approval.)

Property Exercise 4

Our ref JE| your initials

Mr and Mrs T Gregson
49 Silver Birch Ave
Midsomer Norton
BATH
BA3 2LJ

Top plus 2 please. One for Accounts Department and one for File. Indicate routing.

Dear Mr and Mrs Gregson

RE: 75 PARKLAND WAY AND 49 SILVER BIRCH AVE

I am pleased to confirm I have completed your sale and purchase and enclose herewith our receipted Bills and Completion (Statement) together with a cheque for £1,281.44 being the balance due to you. // ~~Following completion,~~ I will now deal with ~~the~~ registration of the purchase docs. When ~~I am in receipt of them~~ they have been returned to me by HM Land Registry they will be lodged (for the duration of your mortgage) (with your Building Society).

If I can be of any further service to you in the future, please do not hesitate to contact me.

Yours sncly

John Edwards

Property Exercise 5

Double linespacing except where indicated

leave at least 3cms horizontal space at each point

THIS CONVEYANCE is made the day of One thousand nine hundred

and BETWEEN HENRY BOSTON and HAROLD CLARKE of 21 High West Street Midsomer Norton in the County of Somerset (hereinafter called "the Vendors") of the one part and JOHN ALEXANDER BRENT of 58 Coronation Drive, Bath in the County of Somerset (hereinafter called "the Purchaser") of the other part

WHEREAS

1 The Vendors are seised of the property hereby conveyed for an est in fee simple in possession upon trust to sell the same

2 The Vendors in exercise of the said trust for sale have agreed with the Pchsr for the sale to him for the sum of Eight thousand five hundred and sixty pounds of the free simple of the property hereby conveyed subject as hereinafter mentioned but otherwise free from incumbrances

NOW THIS DEED WITNESETH as follows:-

1 IN pursuance of the said agreement and in consideration of the sum of EIGHT THOUSAND FIVE HUNDRED AND SIXTY POUNDS (£8,560.00) paid by the Purchaser to the Vendors (the receipt of which sum the Vendors hereby acknowledge) the Vendors as trustees hereby convey unto the Purchaser ALL THAT plot of land situate at the Vendors' Riverside Park Estate in the Parish of Midsomer Norton in the County of Somerset and for the purpose of identifi9cation only delineated on the plan annexed hereto and thereon edged red and numbered 48 TOGETHER with the rights and easements mentioned in the First Schedule hereto but EXCEPT AND RESERVING unto the Venders or other persons entitled thereto the rights and easements mentioned in the Second Schedule hereto TO HOLD the same unto the Purchaser in fee simple

subject to the existing exception and reservation or exceptions and reservations as to mines and minerals with the rights relating thereto and other rights as heretofore excepted and reserved and subject also to the rights and reservations contained in a Conveyance dated the eighteenth day of October one thousand nine hundred and ninety seven and made between the Vendors of the one part and Oil Exploration Limited of the other part and the covts on the part of the Vendors therein contained so far as the same relate to the property hereby conveyed but with the benefit of the covenants on the part of Oil Exploration Limited therein contained so far as aforesaid

2 THE Purchaser hereby further covenants with the Vendors that he will at all times hereafter observe the covenants on the part of the Vendors contained in the said conveyance dated the eighteenth day of October one thousand nine hundred and ninety seven so far as the same relate to the property hereby conveyed and will keep the Vendors and their personal representatives effectually indemnified against all actions proceedings costs claims and demands in respect of the said covenants or any of them so far aforesaid and perform

3 PROVIDED ALWAYS AND IT IS HEREBY AGREED AND DECLARED as follows:-

a) That the Purchaser shall not be entitled to any right of light or air which shall restrict or interfere with the free use of any other part of the said Building Estate for building or any other purpose

b) That nothing herein contained shall operate to impose upon the Vendors any restriction of their right to release or vary any of the covenants stipulations and restrictions herein contained or from selling or otherwise dealing with the whole or any part of their said Building Estate for the time being remaining unsold in any manner as they may think fit

or the persons deriving title under them

Property Exercise 5 continued

c) That all boundary fences separating the plot of land hereby conveyed from any adjoining plots of land on the said Building Estate shall be party fences and shall be repaired and maintained accordingly

4 IT IS HEREBY CERTIFIED that the transaction hereby effected does not form part of a larger transaction or a series of transactions in respect of which the amount or value or the aggregate amount or value of the consideration exceeds

IN WITNESS whereof the parties hereto have hereunto set their hands and seals the day and year first before written

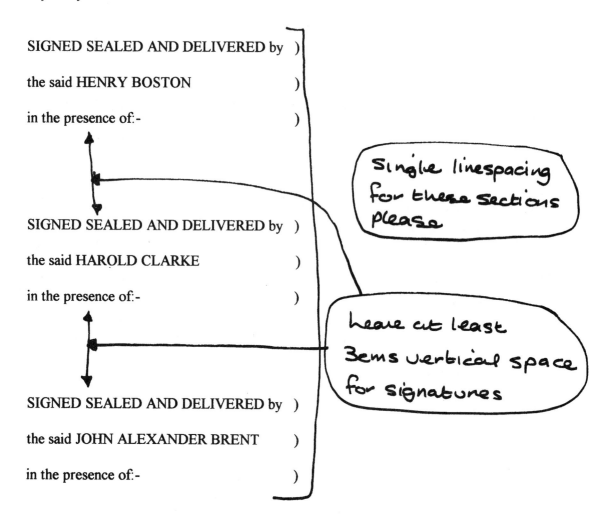

SIGNED SEALED AND DELIVERED by)
the said HENRY BOSTON)
in the presence of:-)

Single linespacing for these sections please

SIGNED SEALED AND DELIVERED by)
the said HAROLD CLARKE)
in the presence of:-)

Leave at least 3ems vertical space for signatures

SIGNED SEALED AND DELIVERED by)
the said JOHN ALEXANDER BRENT)
in the presence of:-)

Property Exercise 6

Double linespacing throughout

THE FIRST SCHEDULE

(Rights granted to the Purchaser)

1 The right (in common as aforesaid) to the free passage and running of water and soil from the said plot of land hereby conveyed and water petroluem products and electricity to the said plot of land through the drains water pipes oil pipes and electricity cables (as the case may be) constructed and laid or within twenty one years of the date hereof to be constructed and laid in or upon the said Building Estate paying a fair and proportionate part (according to user)

2 The right for the Purchaser and his successors' in title owners and occupiers for the time being of the property hereby conveyed and his and their undertenents and servants in common with the Vendors and all other persons for the time being having the like right at all times and for all purposes with or without horses carts or other vehicles me3chanically propelled or otherwise to pass and repass over and along the estate roads leading to and from the plot of land hereby conveyed and Chilcompton Road

of the expense of repairing and maintaining the same

THE SECOND SCHEDULE

(Rights reserved)

1 The right to lay construct and maintain in through or upon the said plot of land all such drains water pipes oil pipes and other services as may be required for the proper development of

Property Exercise 6 continued

the said Building Estate the Vendors and their successors in title making good all damage occasioned by the exercise of such rights

2 The right (in common with the Purchaser and his successors in title owners and occupiers for the time being of the plot of land hereby conveyed) to the free passage and running of water and soil and petroleum products and electricity respectively through the drains water pipes oil pipes and electricity cables constructed and laid or within twenty one years of the date hereof to be constructed and laid or relaid in through the said plot of land the Vendors and their successors in title paying a fair and proportionate part (according to user) of the expense of repairing and maintaining the same

3 The full right and liberty for the South Western Electricity Board to place replace repair renew inspect and maintain underground electric lines and the conduits or pipes for containing the same and groundmounted multi-service pillars in and under or on the plot of land hereby conveyed and overhead electric lines and the poles struts stays and other apparatus connected therewith for supporting the same in and over the said plot of land hereby conveyed and for the purpose of the exercise of such rights aforesaid to enter and break up the surface of the said land doing as little damag as possible and restoring the surface thereon as soon as may be to the reasonable satisfaction of the Purchaser

4 The right to enter upon the said plot of land and plant therein a tree or shrub in accordance with the relevant condition of the Planning Permission relating to the said Building Estate

Property Exercise 7

Use the Completion Statement form on page 107 to complete this exercise.

(Please complete the form)

Statement made out to Mr and Mrs T Gregson in connection with the sale of 49 Silver Birch Ave, Midsomer Norton – date the form with today's date.

Sale price of the property		£93,000.00
<u>Less</u>		
Edwards, Brook and Cole costs	£245.00	
VAT thereon	48.12	
Selling Agents' commission and VAT	1,286.62	
Amount required to redeem 1st mortgage	16,994.07	
Amount required to redeem 2nd mortgage	10,355.03	
		£28,958.84
BALANCE DUE TO YOU ON COMPLETION		£64,041.16

(Emphasise this line and total)

JE1DE352

Property Exercise 8

Use the Completion Statement form on page 108 to complete this exercise.

Please complete the form

Statement made out to Mr and Mrs T Gregson for the purchase of 45 Parkland Way, Midsomer Norton – this was £93,500.00.

They have paid £84.50 leaving a balance of £93,412.50.

Please add the following costs:

Edwards, Brook and Cole costs	£275.00
VAT thereon	48.12
Telegraphic Transfer fee	22.00
VAT thereon	3.85
Coal Board search	35.25
Local search	64.00
Official search	4.00
Stamp Duty	735.00
Land Registry fee	160.00

Balance £94,759.22

Put in the total of the costs – £1,347.22 in the correct place.

Gross Mortgage Advance £32,000.00 leaving a total of £62,759.72.

Reconcilliation Statement

Balance due to you on Sale	64,041.16
Balance due from you on Purchase	62,759.72

BALANCE DUE TO YOU ON COMPLETION £1,281.44

JE/1DB353
Date as today

Probate

You work as a legal secretary to Jenny Brook (senior partner) and Paul White (partner) in the Probate Department. The work in this department is related to wills, inheritance tax and other matters associated with wills including cases where people die intestate (without leaving a will).

The documents you are likely to come across in this department are:

- Wills – these are documents in which a person states his or her wishes about who should inherit his or her property after his or her death. They are usually typed and spaces left for signatures – of the testator and of the witnesses – and for inserting the date that it has been signed.
- Codicils – these are additions to a will. These are usually typed and spaces left for signatures and the date.
- Letters of Administration and Grants of Probate – these are necessary for the release of any funds or property which will form part of the deceased's estate. They are granted to the person, or people, who prove the will – letters of administration only to someone other than an executor and grants of probate only to the executor/s.
- Standard documents such as letters and memos – these will be similar to letters and memos that you would type in any other office. However, the language is likely to be more complex.

In the course of your work in this department you may come across some abbreviations which you are not familiar with. The most likely ones are listed below, and you should always type them in full.

codl	codicil	an appendix to a will
freehd(s)	freehold(s)	the holding of land or a property in absolute ownership

New words that you may come across in this department are listed below with their meanings and derivations.

Accrue	Grow	
Administrator	A person who manages a legal estate for someone who dies without leaving an executor	administration administratrix (female)
Appoint	To choose a person for a task	appointee appointment
Appropriation	Taking	
Beneficiary	Someone who gains money, property, etc from a will (or a trust)	
Bequeath	To dispose by will of property other than land	
Contingent	Depending on a certain event, eg A says that he will bequeath X to B as long as B gets married	
Deceased	Dead	
Devise	To dispose of real property by will	
Domiciled	Living	
Executor	A person appointed by a testator to carry out the terms of his or her will	executorship executrix (female) executrices
Hereinbefore	Before this point	

Liable	Legally obliged or responsible	
Notwithstanding	In spite of	
Personal chattels	Property other than freehold land, money or securities for money that is not used for a business purpose	
Per stirpes	Latin phrase meaning 'according to descent'. If a beneficiary of a will is dead then his or her children get the bequest instead (and if the children are dead then the grandchildren get it)	
Predecease	Die before	
Residuary estate	What is left of a dead person's property after the debts, funeral costs and administration costs have been paid	
Revoke	Cancel	
Testament	A will	
Testamentary disposition	Transfer of property by will	
Testate person	Someone who made a valid will at the time of his or her death	
Testator	A person who has made a will	testatrix (female)
Unascertained	Not specifically identified	

Probate Exercise 1

Our ref JB/your initials

Mrs Veronica Longhurst
19 Riverside Gardens
READING
RG3 4WH

Dear Mrs Longhurst

re: Your Late Father ← emphasise heading

We are dealing with the administration of your late father's Est on behalf of the Executrix, Mrs Eileen Mountson, and enclose for your information a copy of the Grant of Probate with the Will attached. Under the terms of the Will, you are entitled to three quarters of the residuary est and we will be writing to you in due course. [When we are in a position to distribute the assets]

✓ Your father held ~~300~~ 400 shares from Abbey National and the Executrix would be willing to transfer these shares to you direct as part of your share of the Estate, if this is your wish. Otherwise, the shares will be sold and the proceeds fall into the residuary estate. Please let us know how you wish to deal with the shares.

We look forward to hearing from you.

Yours sincerely

Jenny Brook

Probate Exercise 2

Use the Probate Form on page 111 to complete this exercise.

Please complete the Probate form

Edward James Mountson of
3 Winter Close CHELTENHAM Gloucestershire
died on the 24th October 1994

His death to be recorded in District Probate
Registry at BRISTOL

He had been domiciled in England and Wales

The personal representative of the said
deceased is Eileen Mountson of 14 Stratford
Road Cheltenham aforesaid the Executor

The gross value of the said estate does not
exceed £125000.00 and the net value
of the estate does not exceed £10000.00

Please date the Probate form with
today's date

Probate Exercise 3

Our ref JB|your initials

Top plus 2 please. one for Accounts Department and one for File

Mrs Veronica Longhurst
19 Riverside Gardens
READING
RG3 4WH

Dear Mrs Longhurst

re: Your Late Father ← emphasise heading

We thank you for your letter of ← give date for last Friday
and confirm we will arrange for the transfer of the ~~Abbey~~ National shares to you in due course.

Yours sincerely

Jenny Brook

Probate Exercise 4

Double linespacing except where indicated

THIS IS THE LAST WILL of me EDWARD JAMES MOUNTSON

of 3 Winter Close Cheltenham in the County of Gloucestershire

whereby I REVOKE all former Wills and testamentary dispositions (if any) heretofore made by me

1 I APPOINT my sister-in-law Eileen Mountson of 14 Stratford Road Cheltenham aforesaid (hereinafter called "my Trustee" which expression shall include the Trustee for the time being hereof) to be the Executrix and Trustee of this my Will

and personal

2 I GIVE to my Trustee all my real ppty whatsoever and whosoever (including any property over which I may have a general power of appointment or disposition by Will)

3 My Trustee shall hold the said property upon trust to sell the same with power in her absolute discretion to postpone such sale for so long as she shall think fit without being ~~responsible~~ liable for loss

4 My Trustee shall hold the proceeds of sale and all unsold property and my

ready

money upon the following trusts:-

Probate Exercise 4 continued

2

i) to pay my debts and funeral and testamentary expenses

ii) as to the remaining three q2uarters for my daughter Veronica Longhurst of 19 Riverside Gardens Reading berkshire absolutely but if she shall predecease me then for her husband William John Longhurst absolutely but if they shall both have pre deceased me leaving issue who attain the age eighteen years or marry under that age such issue shall take by substitution and if more than one in equal shares per stirpes the share of my residuary estate which my daughter or son-in law would have taken if she or he had survived me and attained a vested interest but so that no issue shall take whose parent is alive and so capable of taking

iii) subject thereto as to one quarter for the said Eileen Mountson absolutely

5 IF the Trustee hereinbefore declared of and concerning any share of my residuary estate shall fail or determine then from the date of such failure or determination such share shall accrue and be added to the other share of my residuary estate and be held upon the like trust's and subject to the like provisions and powers as those affecting such other share

Leave at least 3cms horizontal space at each point

AS WITNESS my hand this day of 19

SIGNED by the Testator the said)
EDWARD JAMES MOUNTSON)
in our presence and then by us in his:-)

single linespacing for this section

Probate Exercise 5

Use the receipt on page 109 to complete this exercise.

Please complete a receipt

We have received the sum of Seven hundred and ninety four pounds and fifty pence re cash in hand in estate of Edward James Mountson from Mrs Eileen Mountson

Please put the amount in figures in the appropriate place and date the receipt with today's date.

Probate Exercise 6

Use the receipt on page 109 to complete this exercise.

Please complete a receipt

We have received from Mrs Veronica Longhurst the sum of Two hundred and fifty pounds only (re House Clearance - MOUNTSON deceased)

Please put the amount in figures in the appropriate place and date the receipt with today's date.

Probate Exercise 7

2

Our Ref TW| your initials
~~Your Ref~~

The Manager
Royal Bank of Scotland
Bank Street
CHELTENHAM

Dear Sir

DECEASED - EDWARD JAMES MOUNTSON
ACCOUNT NO - 590245WS
DATE OF DEATH - 8th OCTOBER 1997
PERSONAL REPs - MRS EILEEN (MOUNTON) AND
MRS VERONICA LONGHURST

We have been instructed by the personal representatives to apply for a grant of representation to the est of your late customer, named above. We enclose a death certificate for you to note in your records. Please return it to us when you have done so.

Please let us have the following information.

1 Details of any account of the deceased, in soul or joint names, not mentioned above.

2 The balance at the date of death on all acccounts of the deceased, with details of any interest accrued to that date.

3 A certificate of interest paid or credited to an account of the deceased since 5 April last.

4 Details of any standing order or direct debit's relating to the deceased's sole accounts.

The grant will be produced to you when available. In the mean time, are you willing to release to us any items held for the deseased?

Yours faithfully

Timothy Wong
Accounts Department

Enc

Probate Exercise 8

Our ref PW/your initials/ ← Insert 1STO456

Mr and Mrs S Rodgers
The Old Lodge
Camerton
BATH
BA3 4HP

Top plus 2 copies. One for Jenny Brook and one for File

Dear Mr and Mrs Rodgers
Re: Your Wills ← Emphasise heading

I refer ~~Further~~ to your recent call at the office and as arranged I (encloses) drafts of your Wills for your consideration.

In particular may I draw your attention to Clause 6 where you were going to consider giving a number of cash legacies to certain charities. ← Please let me have full details of these to include in your Wills.

I look forward to hearing from you in due course.

Yours sncly

Paul White

Please mark the letter PRIVATE AND CONFIDENTIAL

Probate Exercise 9

Please type in double linespacing throughout

WILL:456:SEPTEMBER 1997:JB/ your initials

THIS IS THE LAST WILL of me STUART LEONARD RODGERS of The Old Lodge Camerton Bath Somerset whereby I REVOKE all former Wills and testamentary dispositions

1 a) I APPOINT my wife Patricia Ann Rodgers to be my sole Executrix and Trustee but if she is unable or unwilling to act then I APPOINT my son Jonathan Stuart Rodgers my daughter Sarah June Rodgers and the partners in the firm of Edwards, Brook and Cole of Stansbrook House The Market Midsomer Norton Bath in the County of Somerset (or the firm which at the date of my death has succeeded to and carries on its practice) to be my Executors and Trustees and I express the wish that one and only one of the partners shall prove my Will and act initially in its trusts

b) in this Will the expression "my Trustees" includes the Trustees for the time being of this my Will and the trusts arising under it

2 If my said wife shall survive me I give all of my estate to my said wife absolutely

3 I express the wish that my body shall be cremated

or fails to benefit herein for any other reason

4 If my said wife dies before me the last preceding clause shall not take effect and the following clauses shall have effect

5 I GIVE to my Trustees all of my personal chattels as defined by Section 55 of the Administration of Estates Act 1925 with the request but without imposing any binding trust or legal obligation on them that they distribute the same in accordance with any wishes expressed to them by me during my lifetime or in any Memorandum or paper in my handwriting or signed by me and to hold any items not so distributed as part of my residuary estate

6 I GIVE the following pecuniary legacies absolutely and free of all tax:-

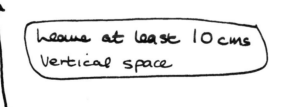

leave at least 10 cms vertical space

7 MY Trustees' shall hold the rest of my estate (my Residuary Estate) either to retain or sell it (without liability for loss) upon the folllowing trusts which are referred to as "my Residuary Trusts":-

Probate Exercise 9 continued

a) to pay my inheritance tax debts and executorship ~~charges~~ expenses and legacies given by my Will or any codl

b) subject as above my Trustees shall hold the rest of my Residuary Estate for such of my children Jonathan Stuart Rodgers and Sarah June Rodgers as shall survive me and attain the age of 25 years and if more than one in equal shares absolutely provided that if any of my said children shall die without having attained a vested interest in my Residuary Estate but shall leave a child or children living at the date of my death or at the date of death of their deceased parent (whichever shall be the later date) then such last mentioned child or children shall take and if more than one equally between them the share of my Residuary Estate which his her or their deceased parent would otherwise have taken

8 MY TRUSTEES shall have the powers set out in the Sched (my Trust Powers)

THE SCHEDULE
My Trust Powers

Centre

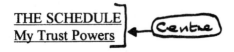

a) to exercise the power of appropriation given them by Section 41 of the Administration of Estates Act 1925 without obtaining any of the required consents even though one or more of my Trustees may be beneficially interested

b) to invest trust ~~cash~~ money and transpose investments as if they were absolute owners beneficially entitled and to pchs retain or improve a freehd or leasehold dwellinghouse for use as a residence by any beneficiary

c) if any of my Trustees are engaged in ~~such~~ a profession to charge (free of Inheritance Tax) for work done by my Trustees firm as if my Trustees were not one of my Trustees but employed to act by my Trustees

d) to insure any property held on my Residuary Trusts against loss or damage by fire or from any other risk even though a person may be absolu8tely entitled to it and to paythe premiums out of the income or capital of my Residuary Estate and any money received as a result of the insurance shall be treated as if it were proceeds of sale of the property insured

e) in their absolute discretion to consent by deed or other instrument to alter the gifts made by my Will on behalfs of any beneficiary hereunder who is under age or a patient within the meaning of the Mental Health Act 1959 or who is unborn or unascertained (or any group or groups of such persons) Provided that my Trustees shall exercise this power only if satisfied that to do so is for the benefit of such beneficiary or beneficiaries

f) notwithstanding any of the Trusts herein or in any Codicil hereto my Trustees may at any time or times in their absolute discretion raise any sum out of any entit;lement from my estate whether vested or contingent and apply them for the advancement and benefit of the bene4ficiary entitled thereto and in the case of any infant beneficiary my Trustees may in their absolute discretion accept the receipt of the parent or guardian of the beneficiary or the receipt of the beneficiary if over the age of 16 years g) To accept the receipt of the Treasurer or other proper officer for the time being of any society institution or charitable organisation benefiting herein or in any Codicil hereto as good and sufficient discharge

AS WITNESS my hand this day of 19

Leave at least 4cms horizontal space at each point

SIGNED by the Testator
in our presence and attested
by us in his presence and in
the presence of each other:-

Insert line space

Witness signature	Witness signature . . . .
Address	Address . . . .
. . . .	. . . .
. . . .	. . . .

Our ref PW|your initials|1STO4S7

Top plus 2 copies. One for Jon Ching, General Office and one for File

Mr and Mrs S Rodgers
The Old Lodge
Camerton
BATH
BA3 4HP

Please mark PRIVATE AND CONFIDENTIAL

Dear Mr and Mrs Rodgers

I now enclose your Wills for your approval. Please read them through carefully and let me know if there are any additions or alterations you would like made, or if there are any points which are not clear.

If the Wills are in order as drawn they can either be signed by you at home or if you would prefer to call into the office to sign, two members of the staff will act as witnesses.

If you ~~would prefer~~ decide to sign the Wills at home it is essential to have two witnesses present when you sign, and it is important that neither witness is a person who is referred to or in any way interested under the provisions of the Wills, or the wife or husband of such a person.

To ensure that the legal requirements are observed, you and the two witnesses should remain together until all three have signed.

When your witnesses are present:-

Insert numbered items here

When this has been done return the Wills to enable me to complete my records. At the same time please let me know whether you would like them to be kept here in our strongroom or returned to you.

I will in any event let you have photo-copies for your records and future reference.

Please be careful not to ~~mark~~ soil the Wills in any way and please do not attach paperclips, pins or staples to them.

Yours sncly

Paul White

Please insert the following numbered items in the appropriate place

1 Write in words the date in the space provided

2 Sign your name (using your usual signature) at the end of the Will where your initials have been pencilled

3 After you have signed, see that each witness signs his or her name and adds his or her address where indicated.

Probate Exercise 11

Our ref PW|your initials|15TO458

Mr and Mrs S Rodgers
The Old Lodge
Camerton
BATH
BA3 4HP

Please mark PRIVATE AND CONFIDENTIAL

Dear Mr and Mrs Rodgers

I am now enclosing photostat copies of your Wills for your records and future reference, together with a note of our charges for your atention in due course.

Your original Wills have been stored in our strongroom, and I confirm that there are no additional charges for this service.

Yours sncly

Paul White

Probate Exercise 12

Use the invoice on page 110 to complete this exercise.

Please complete the Invoice

Please date for today and send to
Mr and Mrs S Rodgers
The Old Lodge
Camerton
BATH BA3 4HP

Our reference is PW|your initials|1ST0459
and the Invoice number is 56843214
(there is no Your reference to be included)

Detail the account as follows:-
To ACCOUNT of our professional charges
in connection with your Wills.

Taking your instructions, drafting and
engrossing the same, forwarding the
Wills to you for approval and signature.

Lodging the signed Wills in our strongroom
and supplying you with copies thereof.

To include all attendances and correspondence
throughout.

The charges will be £100.00 with
VAT amounting to £17.50 making a
total invoice of £117.50

2

Litigation

You work as a legal secretary to Margaret Field and Anthony Turner who are partners in the Litigation Department. The work in this department is concerned with matters involving two or more parties arguing over something. The cases being dealt with are those that are likely to be settled in court. Litigation covers actions in both the High Court and the county court and the procedures for setting out documents and forms are similar for both courts.

The documents you are likely to come across in this department are

- Writs – these are used in cases of fraud, breach of duty and probate, as well as other similar cases, to start the action. They are usually on printed forms. Make sure you are very careful to put in all the necessary information and cross out any parts that do not apply to the case.
- Originating summonses – these are similar to writs and are used in cases of land disputes, inheritance disputes and also many corporate disputes, as well as other similar cases. They are usually on printed forms.
- Motions – these are similar to writs and summonses and are generally used for specialist matters. They are usually on printed forms.
- Petitions – these are similar to writs, summonses and motions and their most common use is to apply for a divorce. They are usually on printed forms.
- Statements of Claim – if a writ has not been indorsed – ie the case fully explained, then a statement of claim must follow within 28 days setting out the facts of the case. They are usually on printed forms.
- Affidavits- these are written statements by a witness signed under oath to be true. They include a statement of whether the deponent (person signing) has any interest in the case.
- Subpoenas – these are commands to a witness to give attendance for the person sending the subpoena. They are usually on printed forms.
- Standard documents such as letters and memos – these will be similar to letters and memos that you would type in any other office. However, the language is likely to be more complex.

In the course of your work in this department you may come across some abbreviations which you are not familiar with. The most likely ones are listed below, and you should always type them in full.

actn	action	a legal process
afft(s)	affidavit(s)	a written statement, sworn on oath to be true
atty	attorney	a barrister or solicitor acting on behalf of another person
(co-)resp	(co-)respondent	a person with whom the respondent has committed adultery in a divorce case
ct	court	a law court
instron(s)	instruction(s)	directions given to a solicitor or counsel
judgt	judgement	a decision made by a court of justice
pty	party	one of the 2 sides in an agreement or dispute
smns	summons	a written command to appear before a court of law

New words that you may come across in this department are listed below with their meanings and derivations.

Bankrupt	A person who is unable to pay his or her debts (ie money owed)
Decree	A court order
Decree absolute	A decree of divorce enabling the parties to remarry
Decree nisi	A conditional divorce
Defence	The case put forward against an accusation
Dispute	Argument
Incapacity	Lack of power or strength
Negligence	Carelessness resulting in damage to the plaintiff
Pecuniary	Financial
Petitioner	The person asking for a divorce
Respondent	The defending party

Litigation Exercise 1

Use the Divorce Form on pages 112–3 to complete this exercise.

The case will be held in the ~~Swindon~~ Bath County Court.

The petitioner, Sarah Ann Baldwin married Martin Charles Baldwin at the Church of St John the Baptist in the parish of Midsomer Norton, in the County of Avon on the sixth day of August 1992. They lived together as husband and wife

Martin is a Computer Analyist and he lives at 5 Cobble Street in York. The petitioner is a Sales Assistant and resides at 214 River View, Midsomer Norton, Bath. There are no children involved, and there are no other proceedings in any other court.

The parties to the marriage have lived apart for a continuous period of at least two years immediately preceding the presentation of the petition and the respondent consents to a decree being granted – this is the reason for the divorce

(4) Particulars – After much unhappiness during 1993 – 1995 they decided to separate on 4 November 1995. The petitioner moved out of the matrimonial home on 6 November 1995 and they have not lived together as husband and wife since that date.

At this stage we cannot insert a cost and you have the details for the Respondent and Petitioner. Use date of typing and complete the Court office address with Somer House, Old Street, BATH BA1 4DT

Our ref MF/your initials

Top plus two – one for Ernest Mullins and one for File. Indicate routing

Mrs S A Baldwin
214 River View
Midsomer Norton
BATH
BA3 2BP

Dear Mrs Baldwin

Decree Nisi ← emphasise heading

We enclose herewith your copy of the form D29 showing your decree nisi. This is not the final decree but you can apply for your "decree absolute" six weeks [and one day] from the date ~~of~~ your d— n— was pronounced.

We enclose ~~You will need to complete~~ form D36 for you to complete and take or send to the crt offices. You will need to pay a fee of £20 to receive your final decree (cheque made payable to HM Paymaster General) or you may pay by cash [or postal order].

If (everthin) is in order you [and your resp] should receive your "decree absolute" (D37) after the six weeks have passed. You will then be free to [re]marry if you wish.

Yours Sincerely

Margaret Field

Litigation Exercise 3

Our ref AT/245/WILSON/your initials

Mr Philip Khambaita
49 King's Cres
DORCHESTER
Dorset

Dear Mr Khambaita

Our Client: Rosemary Wilson
Our client's Vehicle: Ford Fiesta P757 HYD
Accident Date: (insert date for first Thursday of last month)
Location: A37, Grimstone

We have been instructed by R—— W—— in relation to a claim arising from a road traffic accident of which details appear above.// We are instructed that on the date and at the location set out at the head of this letter there was a collision between your vehicle, registration number B412 TYB, and our client's vehicle, a Ford Fiesta, registration number P757 HYD.

It is clear from our instrons that the collision occurred as a result of (negligance) for which you are responsible. In particular, it is alleged that you failed to keep control of your vehicle and drove into the side of our client's vehicle. Full details of our client's claim will follow.

You would be well advised to pass this letter to your insurers immediately asking them to deal with this letter on your behalf.

Yours sincly

Anthony Turner

In the meantime, we look forward to receiving by return your confirmation that there is no dispute as to liability.

Litigation Exercise 4

IN THE BATH COUNTY COURT   CASE NO 98.65874

BETWEEN:

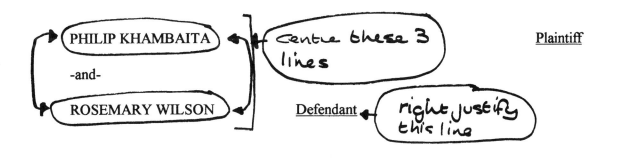

PHILIP KHAMBAITA   Plaintiff

centre these 3 lines

-and-

ROSEMARY WILSON   Defendant

right justify this line

PARTICULARS OF CLAIM

---

1 The Pltf was the owner and driver of a Ford Fiesta motor car, registration number P757 HYD.

2 On * Insert date for first Thursday of last month the Pltf was driving her said motor car along the A37 in the village of Grim stone in the County of Dorset.

3 The Defendent failed to keep any or proper lookout and drove his ~~van~~ car across the road and into the Plaintiff.

4 By reason of the above, the Plaintiff has suffered incapacity, injury, loss and damage to personnel effects details of which are set out in the medical report and statement of damages' attached hereto.

5 The Plaintiff was born on 2 May 1948.

Renumber the remainder of the points as necessary

Litigation Exercise 4 continued

5 In respect of damages awarded to her, the Plaintiff is entitled to interest pursu8ant to section 69 of the County Courts Act 1984.

Emphasise this word

and the Plaintiff claims:

(i) Interest thereon pursuant to Section 69 of the County Courts Act 1984.

(ii) Damages

DATED this * day of 199

Leave 4cm horizontal space (atleast) at each point

(Signed) ....

Change to single line spacing

Edwards, Brook and Cole,

who will accept service of all

proceedings on behalve of the

Plaintiff at

Stansbrook House

T – M —

Midsomer Norton

Bath

Soliciters for the Plaintiff

TO: The Chief Clerk and

TO: The Defendant

Litigation Exercise 5

Use the Summons Form on page 114 to complete this exercise.

Please complete the Summons

The Plaintiff's name and address is:

Ms Rosemary Wilson
14 Whiteways Ave
Radstock
Bath BA3 8JL

and the service and payment should be to

Edwards, Brook and Cole
(You have the address)

The reference can be taken from the letter addressed to Mr Philip Khambaita and his full name and address is

Philip Khambaita
49 King's Cres
DORCHESTER
Dorset

The claim is for - Damages for personal injury and pecuniary loss incurred.

Put "See separate particulars" in the box "Particulars of the Plaintiff's claim" and her claim will be worth £5,000 or less and she would like the case decided by trial.

Put a ✓ in the last two boxes as applicable

2

Corporate Services

You work as a legal secretary to Andrew Cole who is the senior partner in the Corporate Services Department. The work in this department includes matters relating to starting a company, the registration of companies, including Articles of Association, shares, meetings and dissolution of companies, etc.

The documents you are likely to come across in this department are:

- Registrar of Companies Forms – these are used to register a company with the Department of Trade and Industry. They are usually printed forms and care needs to be taken to complete them correctly.
- Memoranda of Association – these are documents in which the subscribers state their intention to form a company. It usually includes a table in which the names and addresses, descriptions and number of shares of each subscriber are listed. The document needs to be signed by each subscriber.
- Agendas and Minutes – these are similar to agendas and minutes in other offices, although they may be more formal.
- Standard documents such as letters and memos – these will be similar to letters and memos that you would type in any other office. However, the language is likely to be more complex.

In the course of your work in this department you may come across some abbreviations which you are not familiar with. The most likely ones are listed below, and you should always type them in full.

decln	declaration	a legal announcement
staty	statutory	requirements by law that have been passed by Act of Parliament

New words that you may come across in this department are listed below with their meanings and derivations.

Grievance	A real or imaginary wrong regarded as grounds for complaint
Remuneration	Reward, payment for work, service, etc

Corporate Services Exercise 1

Our ref AC/546721/your initials

Top plus two – one for ~~General Office~~ David Body and one for file. Indicate routing

Mrs G Lewis
4 Station Crossing
Midsomer Norton
BATH
BA3 2PB

Dear Mr Lewis and Mr Body

Lewis Precision Mouldings Ltd ← emphasise heading (PRECISION)

~~Further to~~ In our recent discussions concerning your wish to form a private company limited by shares, we suggested it would be benefl to hold a meeting. This letter confirms the date of this meeting which is to be held on (insert 1st working day of the month after next) when the M—— of A—— will be completed and details will be given to you for your first Directors' meeting.

In the meantime if there are any other matters you would like to discuss, please contact me.

Yours sincerely

Andrew Cole

2

Corporate Services Exercise 2

(Double linespacing)

ITEMS FOR DISCUSSION AT FIRST DIRECTORS' MEETING

It will be necessary for all of the directors' to be present, and one should take the chair.

Official minutes ~~and an agenda~~ must be taken together with a record of those attending

the meeting.

documentation

The following ~~details~~ should be prepared for presentation to the meeting:-

(new numbered item)
The Certificate of Incorporation of the Company (under No 546721)
dated (leave space of at least 4cms)

1 a copy of the Memorand8um and Articles of Association of the Company as

registered

2 a copy of Form 10, the state ment required under section 10(2) Companies Act 1985 signed by the subscribers to the Memorandum of Association containing:

(i) particulars of the first Directors of the Co — and the first Secretary of the Company and their respective consents to act in the relevant capacity; and

(ii) particulars of the intended situation of the registered office of the Company.

3 David Body and Gerald Lewis, having subscribed to the memorandum and Articles

of Asssociation for one ordinary share of £1 each, must be allotted and issued with one

share and a certificate in respect of such shares

4 A Chairman of the Directors ~~must be elected~~ should be appointed

5 a bank account for the Company must be opened with a bank to be agreed

6 to keep a register of Directors' interests in shar4es or debentures of the Company at

the registered office of the Company

7 ~~8~~ Auditors of the Company must be appointed and their remuneration agreed by the

board ~~and all~~ All (new numbered item) necessary forms for filing with the Registrar of Companies will need to be

accounted for including:-

Certain items will need to be resolved at the meeting:-

(i) Form G88(2) (Return of allotments of shares)

Corporate Services Exercise 3

Use the Memorandum of Association form on page 116 to complete this exercise.

2

Complete form

Insert Lewis Precision Mouldings in heading and item 1.

Leave signature lines blank

The subscribers are:-

(2) David Body of The Old Rectory ~~Stratton~~ Stratton on the Fosse Bath BA3 5XL and

(1) Gerald Lewis who lives at 4 Station Crossing Midsomer Norton Bath BA3 2PB

They each have one share. Please insert total.

Please insert 1st working day of the month after next for date

Witness details are not yet known.

General Office

As an experienced legal secretary, you are working under sub-contract in the General Office – a department that handles work for all the other departments. The work in this department is concerned with general matters, including billing of clients and payment of fees and may involve work on any matters handled by the practice.

The documents that you may come across in this department are:

- Any document from another department
- Standard documents such as letters and memos – these will be similar to letters and memos that you would type in any other office. However, the language is likely to be more complex.

In the course of your work in this department you may come across some abbreviations which you are not familiar with. The most likely ones are listed below for your information, and you should always type them in full.

agmt(s)	agreement(s)	a legally binding contract between 2 parties
tency	tenancy	an agreement between 2 parties on the use of land or a building by a tenant, for which rent is paid to the landlord

New words that you may come across in this department are listed below with their meanings and derivations.

Arbitration	Settlement of a dispute by a third party (or parties) instead of in court
Authorise	Permit/allow
Designate	Give a name to
In reversion expectant	The person who will regain a property at a certain time, eg at the end of a lease or on someone's death
Relinquish	Surrender or renounce
Renounce	Give up

General Office Exercise 1

Our ref TL/ your initials

(date of typing)

Mr N Jackson and Ms S Wong
38 Tulip Way
SPALDING
Lincolnshire
PE11 4TA

Dear Mr Jackson and Ms Wong

Shorthold Tenancy of 38 Tulip Way Spalding Lincolnshire

We act for Mrs D Smith in respect of the proposed Short hold Tenancy of the above property. We understand that the tenancy is to commence on *
We are informed that the rent is to amount to £ per month, and that a deposit has been paid of £9000 and that the term is to be for one year.

leave at least 2cms horizontal space

also

We enclose the Counterpart Shorthold Agreement for ~~your signatures~~ you to sign. Please sign this in your usual signature, where shown, in the presence of an independent witness (not a member of the family). The witness should sign in his or her normal signature and also add address and occupation. Then, please return this to us before the term is to start on *

We enclose a Notice of Shorthold Tenancy in ~~triplicate.~~ ~~duplicate~~ Please sign and date one copy where shown and then return this to us before the tenancy starts on *

his or her

Yours sincerely

Tina Longworth

Please note that you should let us have all of the items referred to above before * as failure to do so may mean that the tenancy is delayed or does not proceed at all

* insert date for 1st Monday of the month after next at each point marked with *

General Office Exercise 2

Double linespacing except where indicated

HOUSING ACT 1988 SECTION 20

NOTICE OF ASSURED SHORTHOLD TENANCY

Centre this heading

1 Please write clearly in ~~black~~ blue ink.

2 If there is any thing you do not understand you should get advice from a Sol or a Citizens Advice Bureau, before you agree to the tency.

Renumber numbered items as necessary

This document is important, keep it in a safe place — emphasise

To 38 Tulip Way, SPALDING, Lincolnshire

of Mr Neil Jackson and Ms Serena Wong

3 You are proposing to take a tenancy of a dwelling known as 38 T — insert address

from   to

leave at least 7cms horizontal space

4 This Notice is to tell you that your ~~Your~~ tenancy is to be an A-S-T. Provided you keep to the terms of the tenancy, you are entitled to remain in the dwelling for at least the first six months of the fixed period agreed at the start of the tenancy. At the end of the period, depending on the terms of the tenancy, the Landlord may have the right to reposssession if she/~~he~~ wants.

3 The Landlord must give this Notice to the Tenant before an Assured Shorthold Tenancy is granted. It does not commit the Tenant to take the tenancy.

General Office Exercise 2 continued

(New numbered item)

The rent for this tenancy is the rent we have agreed. However, you have the right to apply to a rent assessment committee for a determination of the rent which the committee (considers') might reasonably be obtained under the tenancy. If the committee considers (i) that there is a sufficient number of similar properties in the locality let on tenancies and that (ii) the rent we have agreed is significantly higher than the rent which might reasonably be obtained having regard to the level of rents for other assured tenancies in the locality, it will determine a rent for the tenancy. That rent will be the legal maximum you can be required to pay from the date the committee directs.

(✓) 5 This Notice was ~~issued~~ served on (insert date of typing)

To be signed by the Landlord or his or her agent (someone acting for him/her).

If there are joint landlords each must sign, unless one signs on behalf of the rest with (there) agreement.

Dated (insert date of typing)

Signed

(Single linespacing for this section only)

Edwards, Brook and Cole, Solicitors, Stansbrook House, The Market, Midsomer

Norton, Bath for the Landlord.

Received this notice of which this is a copy

Date (leave blank)

Signed

(insert names of tenants below space for signatures)

General Office Exercise 3

DRAFT — Double linespacing except where indicated

THIS AGREEMENT is made the day of one thousand nine hundred and ninety eight

(leave at least 4cms horizontal space at each point)

BETWEEN DOROTHY SMITH of 15 Cloister Way WELLS Somerset (hereinafter called "the Landlord") of the one part and **NEIL JACKSON and SERENA WONG both of 38 Tulip Way SPALDING Lincolnshire** (hereinafter called "the Tenant" of the other part

WHEREBY IT IS AGREED:- (Centre this heading)

1 The Landlord lets and the Tenant takes the dwellinghouse situate at and being known as 38 Tulip Way Spalding Lincolnshire and the garden carport and garage thereof (where applicable) together with the fixtures and fittings and effects therein (in accordance with the Inventory attached hereto) for a certain term of 12 months commencing on the * (emphasise) subject as hereinafter provided at a rent of £ for every month payable in advance the first to be made on * together with a deposit of £900 such deposit to be returned to the Tenant at the expiry of the tenancy provided that no damage has been caused to the ppty or to the fixtures and fittings therein

(leave at least 2cms horizontal space)

2 The Tenant hereby agrees with the Landlord as follows:-

(a) To pay the rent to the Landlord at the times and in the manner aforesaid

(b) To pay as and when they fall due all rates taxes duties assessments impositions and outgoings which are now or which may at any time hereafter be assessed charged or imposed upon the property or on the owner or occupier in respect thereof

(c) To pay for all gas and power which shall be consumed or supplied on or to the property during the tenancy and the amount of all charges made for the use of the telephone (if any) on the property during the tenancy or a proper proportion of the amount of the rental or other recurring charges to be assessed according to the duration of the tenancy

(and electric light)

(d) Not to damage or injure the property or make any alteration in or addition to it

(e) To preserve the fixtures and fittings from being destroyed or damaged and not to remove any of them from the property

(Adjust lettered paragraphs accordingly)

~~(d)~~ To keep the property at all times during the tenancy in a good complete and clean state of repair order and condition and to pay for the repair of or to replace all such items of the fixtures and fittings as shall be broken lost damaged or destroyed during the tenancy (reasonable wear and tear excepted)

(e) To leave the fixtures and fittings at the end of the tenancy in the rooms or places in which they were at the beginning of the tenancy

(f) To pay for the washing (including ironing or pressing) of all linen and for the washing and cleaning of all counterpanes blankets carpets and curtains which shall have soiled during the tenancy (the reasonable use thereof to be allowed for)

(including ironing and pressing)

(g) To permit the Landlord or his servants or agents at reasonable hours in the daytime to enter the property to view the state and condition thereof

( ) Not to assign the tenancy and not to sublet or part with possession of the whole or any part of the property

* insert date for 1st Monday of the month after next at each point marked with *

General Office Exercise 3 continued

(h) Not to carry on or permit to be carried on the property any profession trade or business or let apartments or receive paying guests on the property or place or exhibit any notice board or notice on the property or use the property for any purpose than that of a private residence

(i) Not to do or suffer to be done on the property anything which may be or become a nuisance or annoyance to the Landlord or the Tenant or occupier's of ajoining premises or which may vitiate any insurance of the property against fire or otherwise or increase the premium for such

(j) To keep the drains gutter and pipes in on or under the property free from obstruction and the chimneys (if any) swept

( ) To keep all electrical and other working apparatus in good working order

(k) To keep the grass cut the hedges trimmed the pathways weeded and the beds in a state fit for cultivation and not overgrown with weeds and to clear away fallen leaves

(l) Not to keep harbour or ~~permit~~ allow any pets or animals of any description on the property with the exception of a cockatoo

(m) Not to use the property for any illegal or immoral purposes

(n) To permit the Landlord his servants or agents at reasonable hours in the daytime within the last twenty eight days of the tenancy to enter and view the property with prospective tenants

( ) Not to smoke or suffer any other person to smoke on the property

3 Provided that if the rent or any instalment or part thereof shall be in arrear for at least fourteen days after the same shall have been become due (whether legally demanded or not) or if there shall be a breach of any or the agreements by the Tenant the Landlord may re-enter the property and immediately thereupon the tenancy shall absolutely determine without prejudice to the other rights and remedies of the Landlord

4 This agmt is intended to create an A-S-T- as defined within Part 1 Chapter 11 of the Housing Act 1988 and the provisions for recovery of possession by the Landlord in Section 21 thereof apply accordingly save where the Landlord serves a Notice under Paragraph 2 of Schedule 2A to that Act

5 The Landlord agrees with the Tenant as follows:—

( ) That the Tenant paying the rent and performing the agreements on the part of the Tenant may quietly possess and enjoy the property during the tenancy without any lawful interruption from the Landlord or any person claiming under or in trust for the Landlord

( ) To return to the Tenant any rent payable for any ~~period~~ time while the property is rendered uninhabitable by fire the amount in case of a dispute to be settled by arbitration

5 The Tenant acknowledges to have received prior to the date hereof a valid notice for the purposes of Section 20 of the Housing Act 1988 from the Landlord staing that the tenancy is to be an Assured Shorthold Tenancy

6 This agreement shall take effect subject to the provisions of Section 11 of the Landlord and Tenant Act 1985 if applicable to the tenancy

single linespacing for this section only

New numbered item

Where the context so admits:—

(a) "the Landlord" includes the person for the time being entitled in reversion expectant on the tenancy

(b) "the Tenant" includes the persons for the time being deri9ving title under the Tenant

(c) references to "the property" include references to any part or parts of the dwellinghouse garden garage carport and to the fixtures and fittings or any of them

I N W I T N E S S the hands of the ~~aforesaid signatories~~ parties hereto the day and year first before written

signed by the said)
DOROTHY SMITH)
in the presents of)

Make new page and centre all to form back sheet of agreement

DATED **1998**

MRS D SMITH

TO

MR N JACKSON AND MS S WONG

A G R E E M E N T

FOR THE LETTING ON AN ASSURED SHORTHOLD TENANCY

OF

38 TULIP WAY SPALDING

LINCOLNSHIRE

EDWARDS BROOK AND COLE SOLICITORS

STANSBROOK HOUSE

THE MARKET

MIDSOMER NORTON

BATH

Display attractively to fill A4 sheet

General Office Exercise 4

Use the Shorthold Tenancy Form on page 115 to complete this exercise.

Please complete the form

Insert address of property after "dwelling house known as" You can get this information from the agreement

From Mrs D Smith who lives at 15 Cloister Way Wells in Somerset to Mr N Jackson and Ms S Wong of 38 T_______ W_____ Spalding Lincolnshire

Date of possession will be 1 year less 1 day from date of agreement

Date this notice with today's date

Leave "received" date blank and insert names of tenants below space for signatures

Exam Practice

The Stage II Legal Text Processing Part 2 examination offered by RSA Examinations Board tests your ability to produce a variety of legal documents from handwritten and typewritten drafts.

You will be asked to type three documents in one and a half hours. These are

- a letter
- a legal document
- a form to be completed from given information.

In order to pass the examination you must complete the paper within the time given and incur no more than 9 faults. If you incur only 3 faults or fewer, you will be awarded a distinction.

Key the documents in quickly and accurately and use the rest of the time to proofread your work.

Use the date of the examination on all letters and forms unless otherwise instructed.

Use the printed letterhead paper (at the back of the book – pages 106–122) or retrieve the template for the letters.

Similarly, use the printed forms (also at the back of the book – pages 106–122) or retrieve a file to complete the forms.

Ensure you read the instructions for completing the form carefully. Check that you complete all sections. If you are using a typewriter, take care to type just above the dotted lines. Use the capital X or the hyphen key to delete unwanted words. If you are using a word processor, you may wish to use the Find or Search facility to move from symbol to symbol (ie the insertion points). Use the backspace key to delete the symbol and then key in the information. When asked to delete a word or words, use the backspace or delete key to remove them from the form.

During the examination, you should:

- number continuation sheets for letters – you are not required to number continuation sheets for Document 2
- correct any errors which have been circled – these include spelling and punctuation errors as well as errors of agreement
- follow any instructions on layout, eg centring or rearranging text
- follow instructions for leaving horizontal or vertical space – in RSA examinations, measurements are given in centimetres and millimetres only, so ensure your word processor or typewriter is set to use metric measurements
- produce any extra copies that are required for letters – these may be carbon copies, additional printed copies or photocopies
- remember to indicate the routing of these extra copies – use a black pen to do this neatly

- include your name, centre number and document number on each piece of work, either at the top or bottom of every page – if using a word processor, you might like to use the **Header** or **Footer** facility to do this
- ensure the top and left-hand margins are not less than 13mm
- ensure each printed sheet is clean and not creased, and
- assemble your completed work in the order in which it is presented within each exercise.

Note: Suggested answers for the mock examinations are displayed at the back of the book (pages 95–105).

Exam Practice 1 Document 1

(Letter with copies to Probate Dept and File)

Our ref LW/your initials

Mrs S M Jennings
Rose Cottage
Back Rd
Gelston
COVENTRY CV8 2PO

Dear Mrs Jennings

YOUR WILL ← (emphasise heading)

I enclose a dft of your will for you to check. Please do not hesitate to telephone me if there are any matters that you wish to discuss further. [In the meantime I understand from my secretary that you have arranged to visit my office to sign the final doc on Friday, (give date of last Friday this month). I will make arrangements to have the will witnessed.

I look forward to meeting you again then.

Yours sncly

Linda Ward

Exam Practice 1 Document 2

THIS IS THE LAST WILL AND TESTAMENT ← emphasise and centre this line

of Rose Cottage Back Road Gelston Coventry CV8 2PO

of me Susan Mary Jennings ↔ double line spacing

1 I REVOKE all former wills and testamentary dispositions made by me and declare this to be my last will and testament____________________________

2 I APPOINT my husband Alan Richard Jennings to be sole executor of this my will and in case he is unwilling to accept the office of executor or if his appointment does not for any reason whatsoever take effect then I appoint the executors ~~names~~ named in clause 6 of this will to be the executors and trustees of this my will________________________

3 I ~~LEAVE~~ GIVE the painting of the bowl of ~~Roses~~ roses to my friend Rosemary Anne Archer of 184 Warwick Road Coventry CV2 3GH in appreciation of her friendship over many years__________________________________

4 If my husband survives me for a period of 28 days then but not otherwise I GIVE to my husband ~~absoutel~~ absolutely all my real and personal ppty whatsoever and wheresoever not specifically devised or bequeathed by earlier provisions of this will_______________________

5 If my husband predeceases me or does not survive me for the period of 28 days or if for any other reason the gift to him fails then the following provisions of this my will shall take effect____

6 I APPOINT Rosemary A— A— of 184 W— R— C— CV2 3GH and Linda Ward of Noblers Solrs 6 B— S— L— LE3 4ED to be the executors and trustees of this my will ('my trustees') and I declare that (cap) the expression 'my Trustees' shall mean and include the persons who prove this

Exam Practice 1 Document 2 continued

my will whether ~~or~~ as original executors or executors substituted by acts of law or otherwise ___________________________________

7 I GIVE to the parents of my husband Alan Richard Jennings in equal shares absolutely one half of the real and personal property whatsoever and wheresoever that I may receive from my husband within a period of 28 days prior to the date of my death ___________________________________

8 I GIVE all my real and personal property whatsoever and wheresoever not specifically given by earlier provisions of this will to my Trustees upon trust to sell call in and convert into ready money all such parts of it as do not consist of ready money with absolute power to post pone sale and after payment out of ~~if~~ it of my just debts funeral and testamentary expenses and taxes arising out of or due at my death my Trustees shall stand possesed of the net proceeds of such sale calling in and conversion and such part of my estate which is unconverted ('my residuary estate') upon trust for my parents in absolutely equal shares ___________________

IN WITNESS of which I have set my hand to this my will this day of

19 at least 2 cm horizontal space

Signed by the above named SUSAN)
MARY JENNINGS in our presence)
and by us in ~~his~~ hers)

(1st witness)
of
description

(2nd witness)
of
description

Exam Practice 1 Document 3

Use the invoice form on page 117 to complete this exercise.

Prepare an invoice to Mrs S M Jennings of

Rose C— B— R— G— C— CV8 2PO.

Date for the last Friday of this month.

Description: TO PROFESSIONAL CHARGES in

connection with taking your instrns and

preparing your will, sending dft copy for

your approval and attending you on signing

the same

Charges £70.00 and VAT £12.25, making

a total of £82.25 due for payment.

Exam Practice 2 Document 1

Send a letter to:

Our ref JR/your initials
(suitable date in April)
Ms Dina Palmieri
82 Broadway
LEICESTER
LE4 1MN

Mark letter PERSONAL

Dear Ms Palmieri

emphasise heading

POST OF TEMPORARY KITCHEN ASSISTANT

I am writing to confirm that Nobles offers you temporary employment as Kitchen Assistant in the Catering Department as replacement for Heather Peters who is currently absent from work on account of maternity leave.

Your employment will commence on 5 May 199- and will last ~~for 15~~ 20 weeks from that date. This employment may however be terminated earlier by you or Nobles on one weeks notice. [You will be payed at an hourly rate of £4.00 and your hours of work will be 20 hours. You will not be entitled to any paid holidays or pension which your employer provides to its permanant staff.

or sick pay

3

Two copies of the Statement of Terms of Employment for Casual Work are enclosed.

Would you please sign one copy and return it to me as soon as possible. The other copy is for your own retention. Your employment is subject to such rules, regulations and procedures as Nobles has or may make in relation to its permanent staff and copies of such regulations and rules are enclosed.

May I take this opportunity of welcoming you to Nobles.

Yours sincly

Julie Ravenhead
ADMINISTRATION MANAGER

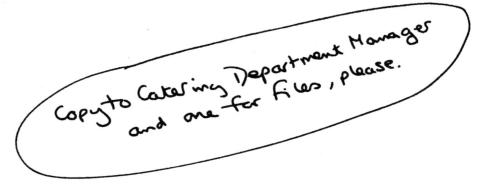

Copy to Catering Department Manager and one for files, please.

Exam Practice 2 Document 2

This line in capitals.

Statement of Terms of Employment for Casual Work

Nobles, 6 Bradgate Street, Leicester, LE3 4ED ('the Employer')

Single line-spacing

1 Description of work

kitchen assistant - to assist with the preparation, serving and tidying up of snacks, meals and refreashments in the staff canteen.

You may be required to do any work within your capacity which the Employer from time to time requires.

2 Dates and hours of work

You agree to work for the Employer under this contt at the times mentioned below:

~~5 May 199- from 10 am to 2 pm~~

End of work period: 12 September 199-

Start of work period: 5 May 199-

Workdays: Mon to Fri

Hours: 10 am to 2pm Mon to Fri

3 Place of work

Nobles, 6 B—— S——, L——, LE3 4ED - staff canteen

4 Pay

£4.00 per hour

You will be paid by check in arrears on Fri of each week unless any other arrangement is noted below:

If for any reason you are indebted to the Employer for any amount the Employer shall be entitled to make a deduction in or towards the discharge of that liability from your pay or any other money payible from the Employer to you.

5 Absences and illness

You must notify the Employer or your immediate superior on every day of absence from work or as soon after as it is practicable and give the reason for and expected duration of the absence and also:

5.2 send to the Employer a certificate of disability by a registered medical practitioner at the end of 7 days from the start of your absence and a further

5.1 Compleat and sign a self-certification of absence doc as soon as is practicable and in any event not later than on your return to work; and

certificate in each successive week of absence

The days which are qualifying days for the purposes of the Social security Contributions and Benefits Act 1992 Part XI are every day on which you are required to work this contt. cap

6 Sick pay, pensions, holidays and notice of termination

None of these are applicable to casual ~~workers~~ staff.

7 Disciplinary rules

See the Employer's disciplinary rules, a copy of which is available from the Administration Manager.

8 Grievance procedure

See the Employer's grievance rules, a copy of which is available from the A— M—.

9 Collective agreements

The terms agreed collectively between the Employer and the General Workers' Union relating to:

9.1 rates of pay; and
9.2 overtime and overtime pay

shall apply to this contt.

↑ leave at least 2.5 cm space vertically ↓

Date

Signed (employer):
Signed (employee):

Employee's name: Ms D—— P——
Employee's address: 82 B——, L——, LE4 1MN

Exam Practice 2 Document 3

Use the Telephone Message Form on page 119 to complete this exercise.

Complete the following Telephone Message, taken by you, on the appropriate form.

Use today's date. The message was from Bharti Mistry for Julie Ravenhead and was taken at 10.40 am. It was about the matter of a JOB INTERVIEW.

The message was: Can attend interview next Mon at 2pm.

Bharti's telephone number is 202 5119.

3

Exam Practice 3 Document 1

(Key in a letter dated 29 July 199- to)

Our ref WM/Stoppard/your initials

Mr J P Stoppard

24 Knight St

LEICESTER

LE2 4WL

Dear Mr Stoppard

(caps)

I confirm that I have prepared a press statement following your instrons.

I would be able to see you on Thurs, 31 Jul 199- at 9.15 am to sign the Schedule and will arrange for witnesses to be available too.

Please contact my secretary to agree another date and time if this is not (conveinient.)

[I know that this is a very distressing time for you and your neighbours but it will be (necesary) to identify any patrons and nominate the trustees in order to prepare the deed. I would therefore be pleased if you could (adwice) me of names and addresses when I see you next Thurs.

(cap)

Please do not hesitate to contact me at any time if you require any further adwice at this difficult time.

Yrs sincly

William Usborne

(copy to Senior Partner and file)

Exam Practice 3 Document 2

SCHEDULE
Press Statement emphasise this line } centre both lines

This statement is issued on behalf of Jeremy Paul Stoppard, neighbour to the families and dependants of the residents of 12-18 Knight Street, Leicester.

(double line spacing throughout)

This appeal has been set up to establish a fund for those injured or bereaved in the terrible disaster at 12 - 18 Knight St, Leicester on Fri the twenty-fifth day of Jul ↑ and their families and dependents. ______

(typist - key in year in words)

The trustees will have discretion how and to what extent to benefit individuals and to determine who are to be regarded as potential beneficiaries. ______

It is expected that within the next few days the names of the patrons and the first trustees will be anounced and that within the next few days they will execute a Deed containing the detailed declarations of trust and the administrative provisions regulating this appeal fund. ______ ✓

It has been decided to establish the appeal as a trust fund rather than as a charity but the trustees will hold on trusts separate any part of the fund which they in there discretion decide is not immediately required for the direct benefit of the victims of the disaster and their relatives and dependants. Such separate trusts will be available to serve comunity needs in ways which commemorate both the disaster and the generosity of those who respond to this appeal; but the most urgent purpose of the appeal is to benefit the victims of the disaster and their dependants. ______

Exam Practice 3 Document 2 continued

[It is the hope and intention that the trustees will be able at an early date to begin distrubutions. As soon as the Deed has been executed a copy will be available at Nobles, Slrs, 6 —— St, L——, LE3 4ED).]

(Anyone who has contributed to the appeal before reading this announcement may, if he feels that it does not meet the purposes for which he has made his contribution, apply to have his contribution refunded. Any such application should be made to Nobles, Slrs, 6 B—— St, L——, LE3 4ED

not later than ~~twenty-second~~ Friday the twenty-second day of Aug (typist - key in year in words), after which date all contributions made will be added to the appeal fund. ______

[The trustees are confident that this appeal reflects the generous and wide-spread public reaction to this terrible disaster. ______

Anyone who believes they or someone they know might be entitled to claim is invited to write in the first instance to Nobles, Slrs, 6 B—— St, L——, LE3 4ED. ______

(at least 2.5cm vertical space here)

Signed by the above-named Jeremy)
Paul Stoppard in the presence of:)

Name)
Address)
Description of Witness)

Name)
Address)
Description of Witness)

(display as shown in single line-spacing)

Exam Practice 3 Document 3

Use the attendance note form on page 120 to complete this exercise.

Complete an Attendance Note for William Usborne, who was the fee earner in this matter. Use the same date as the letter.

The client was Mr J—— P—— S——

and the Matter No is S73954.

The subject was Gas Explosion - 12 - 18 Knight Street, Leicester and attending Mr Stoppard took 8 Units. The details of the attendance were:

To attending Mr Stoppard and advising on the establishment of fund for those injured or bereaved and their families and dependants. Preparation of a Schedule for same.

3

Exam Practice 4 Document 1

Send a letter to:

use single line-spacing for letter

Our ref GN/your initials

Mrs T I Coe
20 Dingley Rd
Great Bowden ← capitals
Leicestershire LE5 2KB

Dear [Mrs Coe]

~~[Matter]~~ DEED OF PARTNERSHIP ← emphasise heading

I confirm that I shall be pleased to act for you in connection with the above matter.

I enclose my firm's Client Care Brochure containing our standard conditions. The additional information you require is:-

1 I shall be responsable for dealing with this matter. In my absence I suggest you contact my ~~assistant~~/secretary [Miss Elliston.]

2 My firms costs for dealing with this matter will be £[100.00] plus VAT and disbursments.

Please will you confirm your aceptance of the above matters and the content of our Client care Brochure by signing and returning to me the copy of this letter. cap

Yrs sincly

GEORGE NICIECKI

Copy

I accept the above terms.

↕ ← leave at least 2cm clear vertically

....

Copy to client (to sign and return)
File

Exam Practice 4 Document 2

CHANGE OF NAME DEED ← (centre heading and underline)

THIS CHANGE OF NAME DEED is made this day of Thurs 13 Nov 1997

BY ME the undersigned ~~Input name of parent~~ Allison Sheila Fearn of ~~Input address~~ 65 Riverway South Bramwith Leicestershire LE9 2LK

the Mother/~~Father as appropriate~~ and Legal Guardian of ~~Input old name~~ Jason Edward Lonsdale-Ellis

now lately referred to as ~~Input new name~~ Jason Edward Fearn who is a

child of the age ~~Input age in years~~ of 11 years whose date of birth is ~~Input date of birth~~ 26 Oct 1986 on behalf of the said ~~Input new name~~ Jason Edward Fearn

Witnesseth and it is hereby declared as follows:- ← (capitals and underline)

1. On behalf of the said ~~Input new name~~ Jason Edward Fearn I absolutely and entirely

relinquish, renounce and abandon the use of his ~~or her~~ said former names ~~if Input old name~~ of Jason Edward Lonsdale-Ellis and on his ~~or her~~ behalf assume adopt and determine to take and use

from the date hereof the names of ~~Input new name~~ Jason Edward Fearn in substitution for his ~~or her~~ former names of ~~Input old name~~ Jason Edward Lonsdale-Ellis

2. The said ~~Input new name~~ Jason Edward Fearn will at all times hereafter in all records

Deeds docs and other writings and in all actions and pceedgs as well as in all dealings

and transactions and on all other occasions whatsoever use and subscribe the said

names of ~~Input new name~~ Jason Edward Fearn as his ~~or her~~ name in substitution for his ~~or her~~ former names of ~~Input old name~~ Jason Edward Lonsdale-Ellis so relinquished as aforesaid to

the intent that the said ~~Input new name~~ Jason Edward Fearn may hereafter be called known or

distinguished not by the former names of ~~Input old name~~ Jason Edward Lonsdale-Ellis

but by the names of ~~Input new name~~ Jason Edward Fearn

(double line spacing unless otherwise shown)

Exam Practice 4 Document 2 continued

3. I on behalf of the said ~~Input new name~~ Jason Edward Fearn authorise and require all persons at all times to designate describe and address the said ~~Input new name~~ Jason Edward Fearn by the adopted names of ~~Input new name~~ Jason Edward Fearn

capitals

signed and delivered as a Deed)
by the said ~~Input parent's name~~) A ____ S ____ F ____
in the presence of:-)

IN WITNESS WHEREOF I have hereunto set my hand the day and year first before written;

Exam Practice 4 Document 3

Use the Telephone List Form on page 121 to complete this exercise.

Please complete a Daily Client Telephone List for George Niciecki. These were for calls taken today while he was engaged.

TIME	CLIENT	MATTER	ACTION TAKEN
9.30 am	Mrs T I Coe 20 Dingley Rd Great Bowden Leicestershire LE5 2KB	Please advise on costs for preparing Deed of Partnership – wishes to open dress agency with colleague	
9.50 am	Mr V Singh on Leicester 240 5512	Mr Singh now has further financial details to be included on his Deed of Separation. Please call back today.	
10.45 am	Mr and Mrs Blackwell on Leicester 256 7133	Wanted to arrange an appointment to sign Dead of Separation – have agreed 3.30 pm next Monday. Have noted this in your diary.	
10.55 am	Marie Sutton of Spencers, solicitors – Leicester 274 4919	Please call back before lunch to discuss new developments in the M Smith case.	
11.10 am	Richard Allen on 01664 67359	Personal matter on which he needs advice. Will be out for the rest of the day and so please call back tomorrow.	

3

Exam Practice 5 Document 1

Ref RH/*your initials*

Mr S W Young
42 Brampton Ave
NOTTINGHAM
NG2 7AS

Dear Mr Young

Re: Account Ref: P- 27 8211-9

We have noted [your request for more time to pay off your indebtedness ~~or that you are now £ behind in your schedule of payments~~] under the above account.

We are prepared, without in any way abandoning or modifying any of our rights under our agreement with you for the above account and until further notice, to allow you to discharge your remaining indebtedness to us in accordance with the following schedules of payments:

Amount	To reach us by
£25.00	6 October 199- and 20 October 199-

You will see from the above that the total amount payable by you will remain unaltered. We do, however, reserve any rights we may have under the agmt for the above account to charge you intrest on any amount to the extent that it is not paid when originally due, and we wish to emphasise that we may discontinue this concession at any time by notice to you, in which event we shall expect you to meet your remaining obligations in full at the originally agreed times.

If you wish to take advantage of this concession, kindly sign and return to use the enclosed ~~[Direct Debit Mandate or~~ Standing Order].

Yours sincerely

Rosemary Dutton
Accounts Manager

Copy to Sales and File

Exam Practice 5 Document 2

(embolden and centre this heading)

HIRE AGREEMENT REGULATED BY THE CONSUMER CREDIT ACT 1974

Office use only: ORIGINAL } (align at right hand margin)
Ref: L-342178-K (single line-spacing)

This is a rental agmt made between US, Charnwood Finance Ltd
having our registered office at S— H—, C— Dr, L— L—, LE11 3JH
and registered in England under No CF9001242-Z AND YOU, the person(s) identified as Hirer below. Where there are 2 or more of you, each of you is separately responsible for performing both your own obligations and those of your co-signatories under this agreement.

SCHEDULE ← (centre and embolden)

Hirer's name(s) in full (surname first): Hart, Robert Henry

Full postal address(es): 18 Wood house Rd, Mountsorrel, Leicestershire, LE10 4YG

Installation name and address, if different from above: Mountsorrel Residential Home, Soar Lane, Mountsorrel, Leicestershire, LE10 3YH

Date of Birth: 28 Feb 1950

Occupation: Propreitor of residential home

Video recorder make: Basco

Accessories: handset

Model: L12 Serial No: JF 80638

Minimum period of hire is 12 months from date of delivery.

Payments (inclusive of VAT at 17.5 %): £34.80 initial payment payable on Hirers signing (refundable on non-acceptance by us or cancellation by you), followed by 6 consecutive monthly rentals each of £24.80 commencing one month after delivery followed by consecutive monthly rentals each of £ 20.80.

(Embolden)

Rental variation: We reserve the right to change the amount of each rental payable by you after giving you at least 7 day's prior written notice of the change. We shall not issue any such notice during the minimum period of hire shown above, except on account of ~~nay~~ any change in the rate of VAT on rentals or for any reason outside our control.

See below for terms and conditions. Use of the video recorder for copying may require consent. Your attention is drawn to the Copyright, Designs and Patents Act 1988. You are strongly recommended to check that you have adequate insurance to cover your liability under clause 3.6 below:

embolden this paragraph

This is a Hire Agreement regulated by the Consumer Credit Act 1974. Sign it only if you want to be legally bound by its terms.

Signature(s) of Hirer(s)

Date(s) of signature(s)

Under this agmt the goods do not become your ppty and you must not sell them.

embolden this paragraph

YOUR RIGHT TO CANCEL

Once you have signed this agmt, you will have for a short time a right to cancel it. Exact details of how and when you can do this will be sent to you by post by us.

SIGNED for and on behalf of

caps

Charnwood Finance Ltd

on the day of 199- which is the date of this agmt.

leave at least 2 cm horizontally

Exam Practice 5 Document 3

Use the Cancellation Form on page 122 to complete this exercise.

Complete a Cancellation form. This will (if used by the client) be returned to Charnwood Finance Ltd, Swithland House, Carillon Dr, LOUGHBOROUGH, Leics, LE11 3JH.

The name of the client is Mr Robert Henry Hart and his address is 18 Woodhouse Rd, MountSorrel, L——, LE10 4YG. His agreement ref is L-342178-K.

Mr Hart will, of course, sign and date the form himself if he decides to cancel the agreement.

3

Proofreading Answer 1

SALIS & BURY
Solicitors
23 Demontfort Road
Leicester LE3 9JR

Tel: 0116 278 4433
Fax: 0116 278 2211

Our ref DH/Minchin/KM
1 date
Allied Building Society
2 18 Marble Rd
3 Manchester
M42 1RY

Dear Sirs

The late Arthur William Minchin
Account Number M969354

I am sorry to inform you of the death on 30 May 1997 of Arthur William Minchin of 34 Archer Avenue, Market Bosworth, Leicestershire, LE12 3TY.

4 I am dealing with the winding-up of his est and enclose a certified copy of the Death Certificate for your inspection.

5 Could you please advice me of the balance in the above account as at the date of death, including interest accrued to that date but not credited, and provide me with a withdrawal form in respect of the account.

6 Please let me know if you require site of a Grant of Representation before
7 releasing any funds and if you require any other docs to be submitted to you.

Yours faithfully

Donald Hickey

8 Enc

Errors

1 The date has been omitted. Today's date should be inserted between the reference and the first line of the addressee details.

2 The abbreviation **Rd** should be keyed in in full, ie **Road**.

3 The postal town should be in capitals, ie **MANCHESTER**.

4 The abbreviation **est** should be keyed in in full, ie **estate**.

5 The word **advice** is misspelt. In this sentence, it is a verb and so should be spelt **advise**.

6 The word **site** is misspelt. It should read **sight**.

7 The abbreviation **docs** should be keyed in in full, ie **documents**.

8 **Enc** has been omitted from the bottom of the letter. Enclosures should always be indicated on letters and memoranda.

Proofreading Answer 2

THIS IS THE LAST WILL AND TESTAMENT

of me

HENRY JOSEPH LAPINSKY of 12 The Ringway Howgreen in the County of Essex which I make this day of 199

1 1 I HEREBY REVOKE all previous wills and codls I have made. This is my
2 last Will. As executers of this my will I appoint my wife Margaret Rose Lapinsky and my brother Barry Charles Lapinsky of The Old Vicarage Main
3, 4 Street How green Essex 2 I DIRECT that all my debts and funeral and testamentary expenses be paid as soon as is convenient after my death
5 3 I GIVE all my estate to my wife Margaret rose Lapinsky of 12 The Ringway Howgreen Essex as long as she survives me by 28 days. If she does not
6 survive me by twenty-eight days I leave all my estate to my daughter Mrs Sandra Ruth Knight of 42 Bishops Drive Saltfleet Lincolnshire

IN WITNESS of which I have set my hand to this my will this day of 199

SIGNED by the above named HENRY)
JOSEPH LAPINSKY in our presence)
and by us in his)

(1st witness)
Name
of
Occupation

(2nd witness)
Name
of
Occupation

Errors

1 The abbreviation **codls** should be keyed in in full, ie **codicils**.

2 The word **executers** is misspelt. It should read **executors**.

3 **How green** has been split into 2 words. It should read **Howgreen**.

4 Numbered points should begin on a new line.

5 **Margaret rose Lapinsky** should read **Margaret Rose Lapinsky**. All names should have initial capitals.

6 The numbers **twenty-eight** should be keyed in either as **28** in both instances or as twenty-eight in both instances. Numbers should always be keyed in consistently within a document.

Note: In the first and last paragraphs of the will, you should leave the gaps for the day, month and year – they would be inserted by hand when the will is signed and witnessed.

Exam Practice 1 Document 1

NOBLES

Solicitors

6 Bradgate Street
Leicester
LE3 4ED

Phone: 0116 254 7213
Fax: 0116 254 8471

VAT Reg No: GB225 1258 35

Our ref LW/*your initials*

today's date

Mrs S M Jennings
Rose Cottage
Back Road
Gelston
COVENTRY CV8 2PO

Dear Mrs Jennings

YOUR WILL

I enclose a draft of your will for you to check. Please do not hesitate to telephone me if there are any matters that you wish to discuss further.

In the meantime I understand from my secretary that you have arranged to visit my office to sign the final document on Friday, *(day, month, year)*. I will make arrangements to have the will witnessed.

I look forward to meeting you again then.

Yours sincerely

Linda Ward

Enc

Copy to Probate Department
File

Exam Practice 1 Document 2

THIS IS THE LAST WILL AND TESTAMENT

of me Susan Mary Jennings____________________

of Rose Cottage Back Road Gelston Coventry CV8 2PO__________

1 I REVOKE all former wills and testamentary dispositions made by me and declare this to be my last will and testament________________

2 I APPOINT my husband Alan Richard Jennings to be sole executor of this my will and in case he is unwilling to accept the office of executor or if his appointment does not for any reason whatsoever take effect then I appoint the executors named in Clause 6 of this will to be the executors and trustees of this my will______

3 I GIVE the painting of the bowl of roses to my friend Rosemary Anne Archer of 184 Warwick Road Coventry CV2 3GH in appreciation of her friendship over many years____________________

4 If my husband survives me for a period of 28 days then but not otherwise I GIVE to my husband absolutely all my real and personal property whatsoever and wheresoever not specifically devised or bequeathed by earlier provisions of this will_

5 If my husband predeceases me or does not survive me for the period of 28 days or if for any other reason the gift to him fails then the following provisions of this my will shall take effect____________________

6 I APPOINT Rosemary Anne Archer of 184 Warwick Road Coventry CV2 3GH and Linda Ward of Nobles Solicitors 6 Bradgate Street Leicester LE3 4ED to be the executors and trustees of this my will ('my Trustees') and I declare that the expression 'my Trustees' shall mean and include the persons who prove this my will whether as original executors or executors substituted by acts of law or otherwise___

Exam Practice 1 Document 2 continued

7 I GIVE to the parents of my husband Alan Richard Jennings in equal shares absolutely one half of the real and personal property whatsoever and wheresoever that I may receive from my husband within a period of 28 days prior to the date of my death____________________

8 I GIVE all my real and personal property whatsoever and wheresoever not specifically given by earlier provisions of this will to my Trustees upon trust to sell call in and convert into ready money all such parts of it as do not consist of ready money with absolute power to postpone sale and after payment out of it of my just debts funeral and testamentary expenses and taxes arising out of or due at my death my Trustees shall stand possessed of the net proceeds of such sale calling in and conversion and such part of my estate which is unconverted ('my residuary estate') upon trust for my parents in equal shares absolutely__________

IN WITNESS of which I have set my hand to this my will this   day of

19

Signed by the above named SUSAN)
MARY JENNINGS in our presence)
and by us in hers)

(1st witness)
of
description

(2nd witness)
of
description

Exam Practice 1 Document 3

NOBLES

Solicitors

6 Bradgate Street
Leicester
LE3 4ED

Phone: 0116 254 7213
Fax: 0116 254 8471

VAT Reg No: GB225 1258 35

INVOICE

Date: *date for last Friday this month*

To: Mrs S M Jennings

Address: Rose Cottage Back Road Gelston COVENTRY CV8 2PO

Description: TO PROFESSIONAL CHARGES in connection with taking your instructions and preparing your will, sending draft copy for your approval and attending you on signing the same

Charges: £70.00

VAT at current rate: £12.25

TOTAL AMOUNT DUE: £82.25

* Delete as applicable

Exam Practice 2 Document 1

NOBLES

Solicitors

6 Bradgate Street
Leicester
LE3 4ED

Phone: 0116 254 7213
Fax: 0116 254 8471

VAT Reg No: GB225 1258 35

Our ref JR/*your initials*

date in April

PERSONAL

Ms Dina Palmieri
82 Broadway
LEICESTER
LE4 1MN

Dear Ms Palmieri

POST OF TEMPORARY KITCHEN ASSISTANT

I am writing to confirm that Nobles offers you temporary employment as Kitchen Assistant in the Catering Department as replacement for Heather Peters who is currently absent from work on account of maternity leave.

Your employment will commence on 5 May 199- and will last for 20 weeks from that date. This employment may however be terminated earlier by you or Nobles on one week's notice.

You will be paid at an hourly rate of £4.00 and your hours of work will be 20 hours. You will not be entitled to any paid holidays or sick pay or pension which your employer provides to its permanent staff.

Two copies of the Statement of Terms of Employment for Casual Work are enclosed. Would you please sign one copy and return it to me as soon as possible. The other copy is for your own retention. Your employment is subject to such rules, regulations and procedures as Nobles has or may make in relation to its permanent staff and copies of such rules and regulations are enclosed.

Exam Practice 2 Document 1 continued

2

May I take this opportunity of welcoming you to Nobles.

Yours sincerely

Julie Ravenhead
ADMINISTRATION MANAGER

Encs

Copy to Catering Department Manager
File

Exam Practice 2 Document 2

STATEMENT OF TERMS OF EMPLOYMENT FOR CASUAL WORK
Nobles, 6 Bradgate Street, Leicester, LE3 4ED ('the Employer')

1 Description of work

Kitchen assistant – to assist with the preparation, serving and tidying up of snacks, meals and refreshments in the staff canteen.

You may be required to do any work within your capacity which the Employer from time to time requires.

2 Dates and hours of work

You agree to work for the Employer under this contract at the times mentioned below:

Start of work period: 5 May 199-
End of work period: 12 September 199-

Workdays: Monday to Friday

Hours: 10 am to 2 pm Monday to Friday

3 Place of work

Nobles, 6 Bradgate Street, Leicester, LE3 4ED – staff canteen

4 Pay

$4.00 per hour

You will be paid by cheque in arrears on Friday of each week unless any other arrangement is noted below:

If you are for any reason indebted to the Employer for any amount the Employer shall be entitled to make a deduction in or towards the discharge of that liability from your pay or any other money payable from the Employer to you.

5 Absences and illness

You must notify the Employer or your immediate superior on every day of absence from work or as soon after as it is practicable and give the reason for and expected duration of the absence and also:

5.1 complete and sign a self-certification of absence document as soon as is practicable and in any event not later than on your return to work; and

Exam Practice 2 Document 2 continued

5.2 send to the Employer a certificate of disability by a registered medical practitioner at the end of 7 days from the start of your absence and a further certificate in each successive week of absence

The days which are qualifying days for the purposes of the Social Security Contributions and Benefits Act 1992 Part XI are every day on which you are required to work this contract.

6 Sick pay, pensions, holidays and notice of termination

None of these are applicable to casual workers.

7 Disciplinary rules

See the Employer's disciplinary rules, a copy of which is available from the Administration Manager.

8 Grievance procedure

See the Employer's grievance rules, a copy of which is available from the Administration Manager.

9 Collective agreements

The terms agreed collectively between the Employer and the General Workers' Union relating to:

9.1 rates of pay; and
9.2 overtime and overtime pay

shall apply to this contract.

Date

Signed (employer):
Signed (employee):

Employee's name: Ms Dina Palmieri
Employee's address: 82 Broadway, Leicester, LE4 1MW

Exam Practice 2 Document 3

NOBLES

Solicitors

TELEPHONE MESSAGE

FOR:	Julie Ravenhead
DATE:	*today's date*
TIME:	10.40 am
CALLER:	Bharti Mistry
TEL NO:	202 5119
MATTER:	JOB INTERVIEW

MESSAGE: Can attend interview next Monday at 2 pm.

TAKEN BY: *Your name*

* Delete as appropriate

Exam Practice 3 Document 1

NOBLES

Solicitors

6 Bradgate Street
Leicester
LE3 4ED

Phone: 0116 254 7213
Fax: 0116 254 8471

VAT Reg No: GB225 1258 35

Our ref WM/Stoppard/*your initials*

29 July 199-

Mr J P Stoppard
24 Knight Street
LEICESTER
LE2 4WL

Dear Mr Stoppard

I confirm that I have prepared a Press Statement following your instructions.

I would be able to see you on Thursday, 31 July 199- at 9.15 am to sign the Schedule and will arrange for witnesses to be available too. Please contact my secretary to agree another date and time if this is not convenient.

I know that this is a very distressing time for you and your neighbours but it will be necessary to identify any patrons and nominate the trustees in order to prepare the Deed. I would therefore be pleased if you could advise me of names and addresses when I see you next Thursday.

Please do not hesitate to contact me at any time if you require any further advice at this difficult time.

Yours sincerely

William Usborne

Copy to Senior Partner
File

Exam Practice 3 Document 2

SCHEDULE
Press Statement

This statement is issued on behalf of Jeremy Paul Stoppard, neighbour to the families and dependants of the residents of 12 – 18 Knight Street, Leicester.______________

This appeal has been set up to establish a fund for those injured or bereaved in the terrible disaster at 12 – 18 Knight Street, Leicester on Friday the twenty-fifth day of July *(typist key in year, eg nineteen hundred and ninety-eight)* and their families and dependants.______________

It is expected that within the next few days the names of the patrons and the first trustees will be announced and that within the next few days they will execute a Deed containing the detailed declarations of trust and the administrative provisions regulating this appeal fund.______________

The trustees will have discretion how and to what extent to benefit individuals and to determine who are to be regarded as potential beneficiaries.______________

It has been decided to establish the appeal as a trust fund rather than as a charity but the trustees will hold on separate trusts any part of the fund which they in their discretion decide is not immediately required for the direct benefit of the victims of the disaster and their relatives and dependants. Such separate trusts will be available to serve community needs in ways which commemorate both the disaster and the generosity of those who respond to this appeal; but the most urgent purpose of the appeal is to benefit the victims of the disaster and their dependants.______________

Exam Practice 3 Document 2 continued

It is the hope and intention that the trustees will be able at an early date to begin distributions. As soon as the Deed has been executed a copy will be available at Nobles, Solicitors, 6 Bradgate Street, Leicester, LE3 4ED. Anyone who has contributed to the appeal before reading this announcement may, if he feels that it does not meet the purposes for which he has made his contribution, apply to have his contribution refunded. Any such application should be made to Nobles, Soclicitors, 6 Bradgate Street, Leicester, LE3 4ED not later than Friday the twenty-second day of August *(typist key in year, eg nineteen hundred and ninety-eight)*, after which date all contributions made will be added to the appeal fund.______________

The trustees are confident that this appeal reflects the generous and widespread public reaction to this terrible disaster.______________

Anyone who believes they or someone they know might be entitled to claim is invited to write in the first instance to Nobles, Solicitors, 6 Bradgate Street, Leicester, LE3 4ED.______________

SIGNED by the above-named Jeremy)
Paul Stoppard in the presence of:)

Name)
Address)
Description of Witness)

Name)
Address)
Description of Witness)

Exam Practice 3 Document 3

NOBLES

Solicitors

ATTENDANCE NOTE

Fee earner:	William Usborne
Date:	29 July 199-
Matter No:	S73954
Client Name:	Mr Jeremy Paul Stoppard
Subject:	Gas Explosion - 12-18 Knight Street, Leicester

To attending Mr Stoppard and advising on the establishment of fund for those injured or bereaved and their families and dependants. Preparation of a Schedule for same.

Units 8

* Delete as appropriate

Exam Practice 4 Document 1

NOBLES

Solicitors

6 Bradgate Street
Leicester
LE3 4ED

Phone: 0116 254 7213
Fax: 0116 254 8471

VAT Reg No: GB225 1258 35

Our ref GN/*your initials*

today's date

Mrs T I Coe
20 Dingley Road
GREAT BOWDEN
Leicestershire LE5 2KB

Dear Mrs Coe

DEED OF PARTNERSHIP

I confirm that I shall be pleased to act for you in connection with the above matter.

I enclose my firm's Client Care Brochure containing our standard conditions. The additional information you require is:-

1 I shall be responsible for dealing with this matter. In my absence I suggest you contact my secretary Miss Elliston.

2 My firm's costs for dealing with this matter will be £100.00 plus VAT and disbursements.

Please will you confirm your acceptance of the above matters and the content of our Client Care Brochure by signing and returning to me the copy of this letter.

Yours sincerely

GEORGE NICIECKI

Enc

<u>Copy</u>

I accept the above terms.

....

Copy to Client (to sign and return)
File

Exam Practice 4 Document 2

CHANGE OF NAME DEED

THIS CHANGE OF NAME DEED is made this day of Thursday 13 November 1997 BY ME the undersigned Allison Sheila Fearn of 65 Riverway South Bramwith Leicestershire LE9 2LK the Mother and Legal Guardian of Jason Edward Lonsdale-Ellis now lately referred to as Jason Edward Fearn who is a child of the age of 11 years whose date of birth is 26 October 1986 on behalf of the said Jason Edward Fearn____

WITNESSETH AND IT IS HEREBY DECLARED AS FOLLOWS:-

1. On behalf of the said Jason Edward Fearn I absolutely and entirely renounce relinquish and abandon the use of his said former names of Jason Edward Lonsdale-Ellis and on his behalf assume adopt and determine to take and use from the date hereof the names of Jason Edward Fearn in substitution for his former names of Jason Edward Lonsdale-Ellis____

2. The said Jason Edward Fearn will at all times hereafter in all records Deeds documents and other writing and in all actions and proceedings as well as in all dealings and transactions and on all other occasions whatsoever use and subscribe the said names of Jason Edward Fearn as his name in substitution for his former names of Jason Edward Lonsdale-Ellis so relinquished as aforesaid to the intent that the said Jason Edward Fearn may hereafter be called known or distinguished not by the former names of Jason Edward Lonsdale-Ellis but by the names of Jason Edward Fearn____

3. I on behalf of the said Jason Edward Fearn authorise and require all persons at all times to designate describe and address the said Jason Edward Fearn by the adopted names of Jason Edward Fearn____

Exam Practice 4 Document 2 continued

IN WITNESS WHEREOF I have hereunto set my hand the day and year first before written;

SIGNED and DELIVERED as a)
Deed by the said Allison Sheila)
Fearn in the presence of :-)

Exam Practice 4 Document 3

NOBLES

Solicitors

DAILY CLIENT TELEPHONE LIST

DATE *today's date*   FEE EARNER George Niciecki

WHILE YOU WERE ENGAGED

TIME	CLIENT	MATTER	ACTION TAKEN
9.30 am	Mrs T I Coe 20 Dingley Road Great Bowden Leicestershire LE5 2KB	Please advise on costs for preparing Deed of Partnership - wishes to open dress agency with colleague	
9.50 am	Mr V Singh on Leicester 240 5512	Mr Singh now has further financial details to be included on his Deed of Separation. Please call back today.	
10.45 am	Mr and Mrs Blackwell on Leicester 256 7133	Wanted to arrange an appointment to sign Deed of Separation - have agreed 3.30 pm next Monday. Have noted this in your diary.	
10.55 am	Marie Sutton of Spencers, solicitors - Leicester 274 4919	Please call back before lunch to discuss new developments in the M Smith case	
11.10 am	Richard Allen on 01664 67359	Personal matter on which he needs advice. Will be out for the rest of the day and so please call back tomorrow.	

* Delete as appropriate

Exam Practice 5 Document 1

Charnwood Finance Ltd

Swithland House
Carillon Drive
LOUGHBOROUGH
Leics LE11 3JH

Phone: 01509 285522
Fax: 01509 471145

Ref RH/*your initials*

today's date

Mr S W Young
42 Brampton Avenue
NOTTINGHAM
NG2 7AS

Dear Mr Young

Re: Account Ref: P-278211-9

We have noted your request for more time to pay off your indebtedness under the above account.

We are prepared, without in any way abandoning or modifying any of our rights under our agreement with you for the above account and until further notice, to allow you to discharge your remaining indebtedness to us in accordance with the following schedules of payments:

Amount	To reach us by
£25.00	6 October 199- and 20 October 199-

You will see from the above that the total amount payable by you will remain unaltered. We do, however, reserve any rights we may have under the agreement for the above account to charge you interest on any amount to the extent that it is not paid when originally due, and we wish to emphasise that we may discontinue this concession at any time by notice to you, in which event we shall expect you to meet your remaining obligations in full at the originally agreed times.

Exam Practice 5 Document 1 continued

2

If you wish to take advantage of this concession, kindly sign and return to us the enclosed Standing Order.

Yours sincerely

Rosemary Dutton
Accounts Manager

Enc

Copy to Sales
File

Exam Practice 5 Document 2

HIRE AGREEMENT REGULATED BY THE CONSUMER CREDIT ACT 1974

Office use only: ORIGINAL
Ref: L-342178-K

This is a rental agreement made between US, Charnwood Finance Ltd having our registered office at Swithland House, Carillon Drive, LOUGHBOROUGH, Leicestershire, LE11 3JH and registered in England under No CF9001242-Z AND YOU, the person(s) identified as Hirer below. Where there are 2 or more of you, each of you is separately responsible for performing both your own obligations and those of your co-signatories under this agreement.

SCHEDULE

Hirer's name(s) in full (surname first): Hart, Robert Henry

Full postal address(es): 18 Woodhouse Road, Mountsorrel, Leicestershire, LE10 4YG

Installation name and address, if different from above: Mountsorrel Residential Home, Soar Lane, Mountsorrel, Leicestershire, LE10 3YH

Date of Birth: 28 February 1950

Occupation: Proprietor of residential home

Video recorder make: Basco

Model: L12 Serial No: JF80638

Accessories: handset

Minimum period of hire is 12 months from date of delivery.

Payments (inclusive of VAT at 17.5%): £34.80 initial payment payable on Hirer's signing (refundable on non-acceptance by us or cancellation by you), followed by 6 consecutive monthly rentals each of £24.80 commencing one month after delivery followed by consecutive monthly rentals each of £20.80.

Rental variation: We reserve the right to change the amount of each rental payable by you after giving you at least 7 days' prior written notice of the change. We shall not issue any such notice during the minimum period of hire shown above, except on account of any change in the rate of VAT on rentals or for any reason outside our control.

See below for terms and conditions. Use of the video recorder for copying may require consent. Your attention is drawn to the Copyright, Designs and Patents Act 1988. You are strongly recommended to check that you have adequate insurance to cover your liability under clause 3.6 below:

Exam Practice 5 Document 2 continued

This is a Hire Agreement regulated by the Consumer Credit Act 1974. Sign it only if you want to be legally bound by its terms.

Signature(s) of Hirer(s)

Date(s) of signature(s)

Under this agreement the goods do not become your property and you must not sell them.

YOUR RIGHT TO CANCEL

Once you have signed this agreement, you will have for a short time a right to cancel it. Exact details of how and when you can do this will be sent to you by post by us.

SIGNED for and on behalf of
CHARNWOOD FINANCE LTD

on the day of 199- which is the date of this agreement.

Exam Practice 5 Document 3

Charnwood Finance Ltd

Swithland House
Carillon Drive
LOUGHBOROUGH
Leics LE11 3JH

Phone: 01509 285522
Fax: 01509 471145

CANCELLATION FORM

Complete and return this form ONLY IF YOU WISH TO CANCEL THE AGREEMENT

TO: Charnwood Finance Ltd
Swithland House
Carillon Drive
LOUGHBOROUGH
Leics LE11 3JH

I/~~We*~~ hereby give notice that I/~~we*~~ wish to cancel agreement ref L-342178-K

Signed: ....

Date: ....

Name: Mr Robert Henry Hart

Address: 18 Woodhouse Road, Mountsorrel, Leicestershire, LE10 4YG

*Delete as appropriate

EDWARDS, BROOK AND COLE
SOLICITORS

John Edwards L.L.B.
Jenny Brook B.Sc (Econ)
Ernest Mullins L.L.B.
Maurice Stand B.A.
Andrew Cole L.L.B.
Catherine Whitby

Stansbrook House
The Market
Midsomer Norton
Bath
Somerset
01761 579731

Memorandum

To

From

Ref

Date

COMPLETION STATEMENT

Name ....

Sale of ....

Sale price of property .... £ ....

<u>Less</u>

Edwards, Brook and Cole costs .... £ ....

VAT thereon ....

Selling Agent's commission and VAT ....

Amount required to redeem 1st mortgage ....

Amount required to redeem 2nd mortgage ....

....

BALANCE DUE TO YOU ON COMPLETION: ....

Reference .... Date ....

COMPLETION STATEMENT

Name ....

Purchase of ....

Purchase price of property .... £..................

Received from you ....

<u>Add</u>

Edwards, Brook and Cole costs .... £ ....

VAT theron ....

Telegraphic Transfer fee ....

VAT theron ....

Coal Board search ....

Local search ....

Official search ....

Stamp Duty ....

Land Registry fee ....

....

....

Gross Mortgage Advance ....

....

<u>Reconciliation Statement</u>

Balance due to you on Sale ....

Balance due from you on Purchase ....

BALANCE DUE TO YOU ON COMPLETION: ....

Reference .... Date ....

EDWARDS, BROOK AND COLE
SOLICITORS

John Edwards L.L.B.
Jenny Brook B.Sc (Econ)
Ernest Mullins L.L.B.
Maurice Stand B.A.
Andrew Cole L.L.B.
Catherine Whitby

Stansbrook House
The Market
Midsomer Norton
Bath
Somerset
01761 579731

Date ....

Received **with thanks from** ....

the sum of ....

....

....

£ ....

EDWARDS, BROOK AND COLE

EDWARDS, BROOK AND COLE
SOLICITORS

John Edwards L.L.B.
Jenny Brook B.Sc (Econ)
Ernest Mullins L.L.B.
Maurice Stand B.A.
Andrew Cole L.L.B.
Catherine Whitby

Stansbrook House
The Market
Midsomer Norton
Bath
Somerset
01761 579731

INVOICE

.... **Invoice date** ....

.... **Invoice number** ....

.... **Our reference** ....

.... **Your reference** ....

	CHARGES	VAT	TOTAL
....	....	....	....
....	....	....	....
....	....	....	....
....	....	....	....
....	....	....	....
....	....	....	....
....	....	....	....
....	....	....	....
....	....	....	....
....	....	....	....
....	....	....	....
....	....	....	....
....	....	....	....
....	....	....	....

VAT NUMBER 879 5532 99

COPIES OF THIS GRANT ARE NOT VALID UNLESS
THEY BEAR THE IMPRESSED SEAL OF THE COURT

In the High Court of Justice

The District Probate Registry at ....

BE IT KNOWN that ....

of ....

....

died on ....

domiciled in ....

AND BE IT FURTHER KNOWN that at the date hereunder written the last Will and Testament

(a copy whereof is hereunto annexed) of the said deceased was proved and registered in the said Registry of the High Court of Justice

and Administration of all the estate which by law devolves to and vests in the personal representative of the said deceased was granted by the aforesaid Court

to ....

of ....

....

It is hereby certified that it appears from information supplied on the application for this grant that the gross value of the said estate in the United Kingdom

** does not exceed/amounts to* £ .... *and that the net value of such estate*

** does not exceed/amounts to* £ ....

Dated ....

Affix Seal here

** District Registrar/Probate Officer*

*delete as applicable

Edwards, Brook and Cole of Stansbrook House The Market Midsomer Norton Bath in the County of Somerset

Before completing this form, read carefully the attached **Notes for Guidance.**

In the .... County Court *

In the Divorce Registry * **No.**

* Delete as appropriate

(1) On the .... day of .... 19.... the petitioner .... was lawfully married to .... (hereinafter called "the respondent") at ....

(2) The petitioner and respondent last lived together as husband and wife at

....

....

(3) The petitioner is domiciled in England and Wales, and is by occupation a

....

and resides at ....

....

and the respondent is by occupation a ....

and resides at ....

(4) There are .... children of the family now living

(5) There are or have been .... other proceedings in any court in England and Wales or elsewhere with reference to the marriage (or to any child of the family) or between the petitioner and respondent with reference to any property of either or both of them

(6) **Reason**

....

....

....

....

(7) **Particulars**

……

……

……

……

Prayer

The petitioner therefore prays

(1) **The suit**

That the said marriage be dissolved

(2) **Costs**

……

……

Signed

The names and addresses of the persons to be served with this petition are:-

Respondent:- ………………………………………………………………………………….

Of ………………………………………………………………………………………………….

………………………………………………………………………………………………….

The Petitioner's address for service is:-

……

……

Dated this ……………… day of …………………… 19 …….

Address all communications for the court to: The Court Manager, County Court,

The Court } ………………………………………………………………………………….
office at }
} ………………………………………………………………………………….
}
} ………………………………………………………………………………….

is open from 10 am to 4 pm (4.30 pm at the Principal Registry of the Family Division - Somerset House) on Mondays to Fridays.

Request for Issue of Default Summons

Please read the notes over the page before filling in this form.

1 **Plaintiff's full name address**

2 **Name and address for service and payment Ref/Tel No**

3 **Defendant's full name and address**

4 **What the claim is for**

Give brief description of the type of claim

5 **Particulars of the Plaintiff's claim**

My claim is worth £5,000 or less ☐ over £5,000 ☐

Total claim over £3,000 and/or damages for personal injury claims over £1,000

I would like my case decided by trial ☐ arbitration ☐

6 **Signed**
Plaintiff or Plaintiff's solicitor

HOUSING ACT 1988
SECTION 21 (1) (b)

ASSURED SHORTHOLD TENANCY

NOTICE REQUIRING POSSESSION

To ....

of ....

From ....

of ....

I give you notice that I require possession of the dwellinghouse known

as ....

on ....

Dated ....

Signed

Edwards, Brook and Cole Solicitors
Stansbrook House The Market Midsomer Norton Bath Somerset
Agents for the Landlord Mrs Dorothy Smith of the above address.

Received this notice of which this is a copy

Date ....

Signed

....

The Companies Acts 1985 to 1989
Private Company Limited by Shares

MEMORANDUM OF ASSOCIATION OF
LIMITED

1 The company's name is "   Limited"

2 The company's registered office is to be situated in England or Wales

3 The object of the company is to carry on business as a general commercial company

4 The liability of the members is limited

5 The company's share capital is £100 divided into 100 shares of £1 each

We, the subscribers to this Memorandum of Association, wish to be formed into a company pursuant to this Memorandum; and we agree to take the number of shares shown opposite our respective names.

Signatures, names and addresses of subscribers	Number of shares taken by each subscriber
1 Signature	
Name	....
Address	
....	
2 Signature	
Name	....
Address	
....	
Total shares taken	....

Dated this .... Day of .... 19....

Witness to the above signatures

Signature ....

Name ....

Address ....

....

NOBLES

Solicitors

6 Bradgate Street
Leicester
LE3 4ED

Phone: 0116 254 7213
Fax: 0116 254 8471

VAT Reg No: GB225 1258 35

INVOICE

Date: ....

To: Mr/Miss/Ms/Mrs* ....

Address: ....

....

Description: ....

....

....

Charges: ....

VAT at current rate: ....

TOTAL AMOUNT DUE: ....

* Delete as applicable

NOBLES

Solicitors

6 Bradgate Street
Leicester
LE3 4ED

Phone: 0116 254 7213
Fax: 0116 254 8471

VAT Reg No: GB225 1258 35

SALIS & BURY

Solicitors

23 Demontfort Road
Leicester LE3 9JR

Tel: 0116 278 4433
Fax: 0116 278 2211

NOBLES

Solicitors

TELEPHONE MESSAGE

FOR: ....

DATE: ....

TIME: ....

CALLER: ....

TEL NO: ....

CLIENT/MATTER:* ....

MESSAGE: ....

....

....

....

....

TAKEN BY: ....

* Delete as appropriate

NOBLES

Solicitors

ATTENDANCE NOTE

Fee earner: ....

Date: ....

Client/Matter No:* ....

Client Name: ....

Subject: ....

Units

* Delete as appropriate

NOBLES

Solicitors

DAILY CLIENT TELEPHONE LIST

DATE .... FEE EARNER ....

WHILE YOU WERE ENGAGED/OUT*

TIME	CLIENT	MATTER	ACTION TAKEN

* Delete as appropriate

Charnwood Finance Ltd

Swithland House
Carillon Drive
LOUGHBOROUGH
Leics LE11 3JH

Phone: 01509 285522
Fax: 01509 471145

CANCELLATION FORM

Complete and return this form ONLY IF YOU WISH TO CANCEL THE AGREEMENT

TO: ....

....

....

....

I/We* hereby give notice that I/we* wish to cancel agreement ref ....

Signed: ....

Date: ....

Name: ....

Address: ....

* Delete as appropriate

Glossary of Legal Abbreviations

Abbreviation	*Full word*	*Meaning*
actn	action	a legal process
afft(s)	affidavit(s)	a written statement, sworn on oath to be true
agmt(s)	agreement(s)	a legally binding contract between 2 parties
atty	attorney	a barrister or solicitor acting on behalf of another person
benefl	beneficial	something that has a helpful or useful effect
clt(s)	client(s)	a person using the services of a lawyer
codl	codicil	an appendix to a will
contt(s)	contract(s)	a formal agreement between 2 parties
convce(s)	conveyance(s)	a document which transfers the legal ownership of land or property
(co-)resp	(co-)respondent	a person with whom the respondent has committed adultery in a divorce case
covt(s)	covenant(s)	a formal agreement
ct	court	a law court
decln	declaration	a legal announcement
dft(s)	draft(s)	a rough copy
doc(s)	document(s)	a piece of paper giving information or evidence
est	estate	all a person owns and is left at his/her death
freehd(s)	freehold(s)	the holding of land or a property in absolute ownership
insolvt(cy)	insolvent(cy)	a person who cannot pay his/her debts (ie money he/she owes)
instron(s)	instruction(s)	directions given to a solicitor or counsel
judgt	judgement	a decision made by a court of justice
pceedg(s)	proceeding(s)	the steps taken in bringing a problem or claim before a court of law for settlement
pchs(r)	purchase or purchaser	to buy/the buyer
ppty	property	items which are owned
pty	party	one of the 2 sides in an agreement or dispute
smns	summons	a written command to appear before a court of law
solr	solicitor	a lawyer who advises clients and instructs barristers
staty	statutory	requirements by law that have been passed by Act of Parliament
tency	tenancy	an agreement between 2 parties on the use of land or a building by a tenant, for which rent is paid to the landlord

Glossary of Legal Terms

Legal term	*Meaning*	*Derivation*
Accrue	Grow	
Administrator	A person who manages a legal estate for someone who dies without leaving an executor	administration administratrix (female)
Aforesaid	Spoken of before	
Aggregate	Total	
Annexed	Added to	
Appoint	To choose a person for a task	appointee appointment
Appropriation	Taking	
Arbitration	Settlement of a dispute by a third party (or parties) instead of in court	
Assign	To transfer property legally	assignable assignee assignor
Authorise	Permit/allow	
Bankrupt	A person who is unable to pay his/her debts (ie money owed)	
Beneficiary	Someone who gains money, property, etc from a will (or a trust)	
Bequeath	To dispose by will of property other than land	
Breach of Court Order	Disobeying a Court Order	
Codicil	Something added to a will	
Completion	When property or land changes hand after signing contracts	
Contingent	Depending on a certain event, eg A says that he will bequeath X to B as long as B gets married	
Covenant (vb)	To agree	
Deceased	Dead	
Decree	A court order	
Decree absolute	A decree of divorce enabling the parties to remarry	
Decree nisi	A conditional divorce	
Defence	The case put forward against an accusation	
Delineated	Drawn/outlined	
Designate	Give a name to	
Devise	To dispose of real property by will	
Dispute	Argument	
Domiciled	Living	
Easement	The right of someone other than the owner to benefit from the land, eg a right of way	
Epitome	A summary	
Exception and reservation	The creation of an easement to benefit the vendor, eg keeping the right to walk/drive across the land being sold	

Legal term	*Meaning*	*Derivation*
Executor	A person appointed by a testator to carry out the terms of his/her will	executorship executrix (female) executrices
Grievance	A real or imaginary wrong regarded as grounds for complaint	
Guarantee	A promise to do something	guarantor
Hereby	By means of/as a result of this	
Herein	In this point/document	
Hereinafter	From this point on	
Hereinbefore	Before this point	
Hereto	To this place, document, etc	
Hereunto	To this place, document, etc	
Incapacity	Lack of power or strength	
Incumbrance	When someone else has an interest in the land, eg a mortgage or a lease	
Indemnified against	Secured/protected against	
In pursuance of	Following/in agreement with	
In reversion expectant	The person who will regain a property at a certain time, eg at the end of a lease or on someone's death	
Judicature	Relating to judges or courts of law	
Land Registry	The Land Registry keeps a record of land and whom it is owned by	
Lease	A contract allowing the use of land or a building for a set time	leasehold leaseholder
Legal Aid	Free legal advice for people who earn less than a certain amount	
Legal tender	Currency that can be used to pay for goods, services, etc	
Liable	Legally obliged or responsible	
Maintenance	The money a husband or wife pays after a divorce to support the ex-partner or a child	
Mortgage	A loan for buying a property – the property is also used as security	mortgagee a mortgagor/er
Negligence	Carelessness resulting in damage to the plaintiff	
Notwithstanding	In spite of	
Parchment	A type of stiff, yellowish paper sometimes used for legal documents	
Pecuniary	Financial	
Personal chattels	Property other than freehold land, money or securities for money that is not used for a business purpose	
Per stirpes	Latin phrase meaning 'according to descent'. If a beneficiary of a will is dead then his/her children get the bequest instead (and if the children are dead then the grandchildren get it)	

Legal term	*Meaning*	*Derivation*
Petitioner	The person asking for a divorce	
Predecease	Die before	
Purchaser	Buyer	
Relinquish	Surrender or renounce	
Remuneration	Reward, payment for work, service, etc	
Renounce	Give up	
Residuary estate	What is left of a dead person's property after the debts, funeral costs and administration costs have been paid	
Respondent	The defending party	
Restrictions	Limits	
Revoke	Cancel	
Seised of	Are the legal owners of	
Situate (adjective)	Situated	
Stipulations	Guarantees, promises	
Surveyor	An official who checks buildings or land in order to give it a price	
Testament	A will	
Testamentary disposition	Transfer of property by will	
Testate person	Someone who made a valid will at the time of his/her death	
Testator	A person who has made a will	testatrix (female)
Thereto	To that or it	
Title Deeds	Documents that prove someone owns a property	
Transactions	Agreements/negotiations	
Transfer	To convey or make over the ownership of or rights in a property from one party to another	transferee transference transferor/er
Trustee	A person managing the estate of a dead person or of someone not old enough to be legally responsible him/herself	
Unascertained	Not specifically identified	
Vendor	Seller	
Whereas	It being the case that; since	
Whereof	Of which	
Witness	A person who gives evidence in a court of law *or* A person who confirms another person's signature	